Intentional Connections

Learning to grow from children

Gloria O'Brien

iUniverse, Inc.
Bloomington

iUniverse books may be ordered through booksellers or by contacting:

iUniverse
1663 Liberty Drive
Bloomington, IN 47403
www.iuniverse.com
1-800-Authors (1-800-288-4677)

ISBN: 978-1-4502-7960-4 (sc)
ISBN: 978-1-4502-7959-8 (hc)
ISBN: 978-1-4502-7961-1 (ebook)

Library of congresss Control Number: 2010918463

Printed in the United States of America

iUniverse rev. date: 2/3/2011

As a licensed marriage and family therapist, I am constantly stressing that parents need to separate their own egos, needs, and wounds from their children. This book is a wonderfully written synthesis of these problems and solutions. It is clearly and precisely stated. The complexities, necessities, and consequences of the differentiation process, or lack thereof, are persuasively presented. I would gladly give this book to any parent, male or female, who seeks answers to questions about parenting teens and young adults.

Certainly some of the most important lessons I have learned have been from my children. They have taught me about myself and the world. As Gloria points out, for those who are willing to listen and learn about themselves, children can teach us well. As my children grow, the advice and the lessons keep coming, parenting becomes easier, and the boundaries between us become clearer.

Well done, Gloria! You have nailed this one. I am proud to call you my colleague and former student. Now you can teach me again, as my students and clients always have.

Susan Carter-Stutzman, PhD, Marriage and Family Therapist

Contents

Acknowledgments

When I was a child, three women opened their doors and simply let me be. It contributed to my sense of self.

Thank you to my family of origin for being the vehicle that allowed for significant stretching and personal growth.

I deeply love the men in my life, Mark, Mark, and Lee, who have been a constant source of motivation and enlightenment.

The closest friends who taught me the meaning of friendship in the simplest and most unconditional way encouraged the writing of this book: Mary Majtenyi and Barbara Brockwell. Thanks also to my support team, who edited, created, and designed it: Susan Carter-Stutzman, Sherrie Nielsen, Lori Luna, and Christine Mulder.

To the women and adult children who contributed to this authorship—I continue to believe in all of you.

Introduction

All civilized societies have consistent beliefs about the relationships between adults and children. Children have physical, social, emotional, moral, and academic needs that change somewhat predictably as they move through the stages of childhood. Adults believe that we must nourish those needs. No one would question that it is our obligation to care for our children. Child care is such an important topic that various holy books, cultures, researchers, and parenting experts offer guidance on the subject. Yet despite all of the knowledge from all of the disciplines, adults do not maximize the benefits that result from having relationships with children.

Most adults identify with current ideology, which suggests that children are vulnerable and innocent, at least in their early years. Because of these beliefs, adults view themselves as children's teachers, mentors, counselors, overseers, and guides. This book suggests that we broaden our current definition of children and consider a different paradigm, which supports the belief that children are capable of teaching us as well as learning from us. This theory suggests that we learn to listen and that we observe our interactions with children more attentively. When we do so, we can evaluate these events with enhanced understanding. We can discover the adult life lessons that children can provide. Before adults can benefit more fully from relationships with children, they must learn about the personal obstacles that interfere with this process. The necessary self-exploration is outlined in the chapters of this book. Each chapter discusses a step adults need to consider if they want to learn more from children. Real-life vignettes are provided that illustrate the concepts.

Because mothers are more likely to admit frustration and seek advice from counselors, the vignettes focus on mothers and their children. These women admittedly felt great despair, as well as confusion. They recognized that they had exhausted the options they were familiar with, and they believed that their parenting efforts were failing. They were lost. As mothers, their emotional bonds with their children created unending determination. At the same time, these mothers were in emotional pain. The desire to alleviate that pain and to hold onto their children became the impetus for changing the way they understood their parent-child relationships. Though their children required parenting, these mothers were able to recognize that their children's issues raised similar or different issues in them. As they parented, they became able to identify opportunities for their own personal growth. Ultimately, these women held themselves accountable for their own thoughts, feelings, and behaviors, separate from their children. Greater insights into themselves, increased connectedness with their children, and a different understanding of their world resulted.

The women in these stories got lost in the details of parenting, which is easy to do. Some experts would argue that good parenting is defined as paying attention to those details. The women wanted their children to succeed, and to that end, this book does not diminish the role of parenting. However, these women were able to temporarily step back from their parenting. They chose to develop awareness of the steps presented in the following chapters and implement them. The concepts are basic psychological principles, but the implementation of these principles requires dedication. These mothers separated their egos from parenting, considered how their pasts interfered with their parent-child relationships, and shifted from emotional extremes to a balanced approach that considered both feelings and logic. These changes demanded greater insight into the self, the willingness to change, and the desire to forgive. My hope is that other adults will identify with their experiences and use them for their own personal growth.

The cases in this book also include opinions from older teens and young adults who were impacted by their parent-child relationships, both positively and negatively. They are unedited vignettes from a younger generation's perspective. Some have learned from their relationships, and some are likely to repeat the patterns already established in their families. All of the contributors told the truth as they understand it.

My greatest pain and most shameful moments occurred in the role of mother. Nothing has ever compared to the helplessness I felt as a parent. However, it is my belief that those experiences lead to profound, personal growth that is available to everyone. We do not have to be mothers to learn from children but simply believe and avail ourselves to the opportunities that exist to learn from them.

It is time to connect children and adults, with children setting the stage for adults to develop as more enlightened beings. Children come to us, and perhaps we choose them so that we grow and learn together, as independent but intertwined units. They are gifts for us, and perhaps they give us more than we realized in the past.

I write this book as a licensed therapist and as a parent who wants to share that our children come through us with a mission to change us. At times, they are a complete joy and therefore make us feel complete. Other experiences can be like nightmares. Bad dreams are akin to a slap in the face, inherently designed to be remembered, and we often awake from them with a rush of negative emotions. But they carry messages from our subconscious that need to be revealed and understood. Children, too, carry those messages. It is through those messages that we can grow. The challenge is to look beyond specific events, become objective observers, and recognize what we as adults need to do to better ourselves.

Chapter 1 — Supporting the Theory

My belief that children have the ability to be our teachers materialized through my own maternal experiences, client observations, research, and other documented beliefs that span theology, psychology, marriage and family theories, philosophy, and other disciplines.

While I was being educated in psychology and counseling, I learned about a paradigm called *systems theory*. It was relatively new (mid-twentieth century) compared to other psychological theories and what made it unique was that it focused on individuals within families. Based on systems theory, different family members might try to balance staying connected to the family with separating themselves as individuals. It is not uncommon to see children move away from their families when they feel that the families are too demanding. It is also not unusual to see an adult child succumb to the wishes of the family even when the wishes appear destructive to the child. Both extremes are considered dysfunctional. Ultimately, the goal of each family member is to maintain a healthy balance of connectedness and individuality.

A common therapeutic treatment involves teaching the client to separate his or her thoughts from feelings, without interference from the family's emotional attachments. Of course, this is easier said than done, but successful therapy results in the client developing this skill. There is no requirement that the child or the parent be the client. Rather, the client, adult or child, is often the most motivated family member. Conceivably, a child could learn to respond to a family situation differently, which might cause a parent to react differently in the family. As an example, parents might eat when they feel stressed. If the child learns to initiate a family bike ride when the family is stressed, the other family members might agree and choose exercise instead of overeating.

Early in the history of the science of psychology, Sigmund Freud placed excessive parenting responsibilities on mothers and consequently blamed them for a myriad of issues including unusual parental jealousies, sexual fantasies, and even autism. However, in the twentieth century a psychologist from Russia, Urie Bronfenbrenner, postulated that children are affected by all types of environments, including the environments provided by mothers. These environments, such as church and schools, have as much potential to impact children as families. Today, it is conventional wisdom that human development does not happen in a vacuum but through exposure to various systems. When children learn in other environments and are influenced by other systems, the opportunity exists for children to share new information in the home. Through those shared experiences, parents can grow from the children's knowledge, and the parents can become an extension of the children. As the children grow in knowledge and experience, parents have opportunities for change.

Some religious perspectives, including Hinduism, Buddhism, and others, have tenets rooted in rebirth or reincarnation. These beliefs suggest that a soul continues on a journey that allows it to enter many physical bodies. These reentries are chosen prior to birth and often allow the soul to work through unresolved issues from prior lives. The past-life actions can be intentional or circumstantial, depending on the religion. Regardless, most religions that support rebirth espouse that the soul makes decisions prior to entering the physical body that allows the optimal environment needed to work through designated issues.

Sometimes, reentries are for personal enlightenment, but human beings also come together to assist others with their issues. The dynamic is not unidirectional between a child and a parent. In other words, not only can the parent teach the child, but the child can teach the parent. As an example, a parent seeking the virtue of forgiveness may have a child who frequently requires forgiveness. Therefore, as a consequence of rebirth, we can learn, correct imbalances of the past, and teach others. Decisions relating to reincarnation include the circumstances in which we will be born, which set the stage for our learning and/or teaching. The reincarnation perspective emphasizes the interactions of these systems for the ultimate development of spiritual goals. Bronfenbrenner related his theory to individual learning and development without emphasis on spirituality.

Christian religions also support the importance of children. The Bible, which is the sacred book of Christian believers, clarifies the importance of children and the interrelatedness of children and parenting for fruitful human development. It is scripted that parents who receive children receive Jesus and that the humbleness of children is necessary for adults' entry into heaven (Matthew 18:2–6 ESV).

Existential philosophy is a belief system that says we must take complete personal responsibility for creating a purposeful life and defining the meaning of our own existence. Existentialists would argue that suffering is a natural and normal part of life's journey and that we can achieve greater awareness and understanding of ourselves through the discomforts, struggles, and choices that present themselves in everyday events. Nothing in existential theory suggests that angst and suffering are isolated from experiences with children. Accordingly, adults who are exposed to adult-child interactions, both positive and negative, have opportunities for self-growth.

Some of us are not rooted in religion, science, or theory based on research. Some of us understand the world based on controversial phenomena that exist beyond the physical. In 1982, Nancy Ann Tappe, a known psychic and synesthete (synesthetes have senses that are not separate; for example, a number might be seen with a specific color or a word might trigger a taste) wrote a book about special children whose births initiated in the 1960s. She called these children "Indigo children," referring to their deep blue- or violet-colored auras, the energy fields around their bodies. Without scientific support, the concept of Indigos has gained momentum around the globe; they have received attention from ABC News, CNN, and others.

Indigo children (also known as Rainbow or Crystalline) are identified primarily by their thoughts and behaviors and are defined by the following characteristics:

- Possess high moral standards
- Readily question integrity
- Have an intellect not measured by standard IQ testing
- Have strong personalities
- May appear withdrawn
- Have a purposeful existence
- Trust themselves
- Are untainted by cultural dictates
- Do not conform to standardized norms
- Rebel against authority when there is perceived injustice

Indigo children purportedly contain different neurological wiring, and perhaps this is why they are allegedly misdiagnosed, often with attention deficit disorder, autism, and learning disabilities, by the medical profession.

All humans contain DNA that allows for individual differences, cell replication, data storage, and evolution. In essence, DNA is the history of human beings, individually, universally, and ancestrally. DNA is surrounded by an electromagnetic field that has the capacity to carry information. In Indigos, DNA communicates in a broader way, which allows for higher functioning.

Does all of this mean that Indigos and other specially labeled children are our future? The claim is that they exist because they are our bridge to heightened spirituality and connectedness. They are a part of a new world order that emphasizes truth, justice, balance, sensitivity, and love. Parents and teachers of Indigos are challenged by these children. However, the message of Indigos is universal in that they were not born to be parented but to exist in a way that is simply meant to be. Dr. Doreen Virtue describes Indigos as "warriors" who are God's answer to our "collective prayers for peace."

These are but a few examples of the interplay between children and adults that support the significance of children's abilities to impact others. However, my favorite example is from a simple yet profound story, *The Little Prince*, by Antoine de Saint-Exupéry. The narrator in this story describes his early memories of drawing pictures with great enthusiasm, only to be discouraged by the adults around him. He recalled that adults never understood and that trying to explain was exhausting. The narrator gave up his artistic dreams, became a pilot, and met the little prince while his aircraft was downed in the desert. The prince traveled to many places before he met the pilot, and through those travels he conversed with adults who were indifferent, pompous, and preoccupied. When the prince asked the pilot for a drawing, the pilot no longer had the imagination or the desire to draw. The pilot thought the prince was a nuisance, but eventually he discovered meaning in their relationship.

Ultimately, the prince decided that what he always wanted was at home, so he allowed himself to be bitten by a snake, freeing himself from his physical body so that he could return to his planet. Before the prince left, he told the pilot that he would be happily living on one of the stars in the sky, there would always be a special bond between them, and the relationship shared would be worth the pain of the loss. In the last paragraph of the story, Antoine de Saint-Exupéry wrote that the pilot waited with hope for the little prince to return.

In 1935, de Saint-Exupéry had been marooned in the Sahara Desert for four days. Admittedly, his hallucinations were severe, but the outcome, an eloquent story of how a child changed a man, was about the gift of friendship, connectedness, transition, and hope. The child could recognize what adults could not: that "matters of consequence" were insignificant when compared to the opportunities of life with love; that the time that you share with others solidifies your relationships; that experiences last forever; that what you see with your eyes is never as important as what you cannot see; and that the clearest vision is through the heart.

Chapter 2 — Redefining Children

The concept of family is a basic social construct. How we fully define it depends on culture, history, geography, religion, laws, economy, and social issues. As with many social constructs, the American family has experienced a metamorphosis since the early days of our founding fathers.

At the beginning of American settlements, family life was determined by immigrant standards from Europe. Early families were self-contained agrarian units; they lived and worked together. A typical family fed itself through hunting and farming, built its own shelters, sewed its own clothing, and cared for one another.

Husbands and wives usually stayed together. Though laws allowed for divorce, it was impractical because an official divorce mandated a return to Europe. Couples did legally separate and live in different dwellings, but without a legal divorce, they couldn't remarry.

Children were viewed as young adults, and it was the obligation of the father to discipline, teach religion, and foster moral standards. Children received informal educations provided by the parents that typically focused on skills for living, such as sewing, spinning, and farming.

This definition of the family was fairly consistent until the 1800s, when industrialization changed our economic landscape.

Children went to work in factories. Trades were chosen early in life, and marriage often occurred during the teen years.

As the concept of work became modernized, cities developed. Fathers went off to work and were less available in the home as industrialization progressed. This caused the responsibilities in the home to shift. Men reduced the time spent on parenting, and women increased their focus on the children's needs. In this period, children were used as labor in factories, which eventually resulted in laws that protected them. As more laws emerged, the perspective of children as undersized adults changed to children as innocent and vulnerable beings. Education norms developed as well. Formal education replaced informal schooling at home, and a new developmental stage called adolescence, or the stage between adulthood and childhood, appeared.

The family was the woman's domain by the late nineteenth century. Experts in many fields believed that mothers were critical for the healthy development of children, but women were viewed as naturally inferior to men; their emotional reactivity confirming their inferiority. Professionals like physicians and psychologists recommended that mothers learn to restrain themselves from exposing feelings for the sake of their own civility and the children. As women educated themselves more, they came to believe the professionals and shifted their parenting styles in accordance with the current thinking.

How the family looks today is quite different from even fifty years ago. Baby boomer children typically had two-parent families, with a mother in the home and a father at work. Families were usually homogenous. As teens and young adults, many boomers were antiestablishment; they viewed war as unnecessary, protested in the streets, encouraged social movements, changed various cultural standards, and engaged in risky behaviors.

Today, the constellation of the family takes many shapes. There are single- or two-parent households, homosexual parents, grandparents raising grandchildren, surrogate parents, foster parents, and adopted parents. Families can host mixed ethnicities, races, and religions. A twenty-first-century mother of a small child is concerned about early encouragement, contaminated toys, dangers in the home, proper nutrition, and autism. She seeks early education and socialization and questions if her child can successfully potty train in a day. Child predators are universally feared; consequently, children no longer romp through the streets until curfew as many boomer children did. There are organized sports, arranged play dates, and scheduled carpools.

Parents of school-age children join PTAs and closely monitor the public school systems. They observe teachers and other students by volunteering in classrooms; they hover around their children and their children's environments. They may demand different teachers, attempt to influence curriculum, and connect with other parents who may provide their children with status.

Technology can be their greatest enemy. Teens communicate privately through computers and cell phones, and consequently, parents can easily be shut out of the teens' activities. Responsible parenting may mean securing birth control rather than risk teen pregnancy and allowing illegal drinking only within the home. Global tracking devices provide real-time locations; parents install computer nannies, monitor social networks, and scrutinize cell phone records, while schools install metal detectors at proms.

Throughout the entire modern parenting process, there is the possibility that a child will call authorities about attempted discipline, lie to those who are required by laws to report suspected child abuse and neglect, or accidentally accuse parents of wrongdoing. Government oversight of children is greater than ever, though publicly funded systems are overcrowded, underfunded, and floundering. The founding fathers of this country would not comprehend parenting in the new millennium. Today, our children seem far from innocent and vulnerable. Children can talk to strangers who are predators, engage in risky sexual behaviors, use and abuse legal and illegal substances, and at the same time, convince their parents that they are following household rules. They remain innocent to outside influences but clever with their parents.

The assumption that children are miniature adults or quite vulnerable presents two different, polarized perspectives. Most adults understand that children develop at different rates and that within one child there can be significant inconsistencies in maturity. No one has the ability to determine how a specific child will react to others; how others will react to the child; the speed at which the child will develop; what the child's strengths and weaknesses will be; and what outside influences will take root, and this makes parenting difficult. Experts can make generalized statements about parenting, but knowing your own child is a parent's greatest strength.

History shows that the definition of family is fluid. The fact that the concept of family continues through the centuries represents its ability to adjust to other influences in society. For the purposes of this book, recognize that previous definitions of children are no longer appropriate. Our current research confirms that children are not small adults. Without a doubt, children are vulnerable to increasing exposure to various threats, but the description "vulnerable" is incomplete.

Children can see the world unfiltered by masks. Young children especially are not concerned with their public images and putting on airs. They are not burdened by societal expectations, unlike adults. Because they are simple and unrefined, they often express wisdom beyond their years. "Out of the mouths of babes" is a biblical reference but also an American idiom that underscores this concept. When we redefine children to include having insight as well as innocence, we can then recognize that they may challenge us because it is their given path in life to do so. Defining them as having insights restructures our patterns of communication with them. It allows us to recognize that they can teach us if we are willing to be taught.

Chapter 3 — Children Are Not Ours

Culture dictates our images of motherhood, and certainly American culture has shifted over the years. There was a time not too long ago when motherhood equated to womanhood. Childless women were pitied. It was common for mothers with adult children to ask when they would wed, and there was a relentless pursuit of grandchildren.

During World War II, many women entered the workforce and contributed to the national economy while their husbands and brothers fought overseas. Rosie the Riveter was both symbolic and real (Rose Will Monroe); a woman who learned that she could do work previously performed by men. When the war ended, some of those women reluctantly vacated their jobs and returned to their homes. During the mid-1960s, Betty Friedan wrote about those women and their dissatisfaction with their culturally dictated lives.

Though times changed in the twentieth century and women gained greater employment and career access, many rituals attached to pregnancy continued. Expecting mothers built the pink nests for girls and blue for boys. Baby showers encourage gifts of necessary (or not) items for the upcoming event, though modern showers might include men and may not be a surprise anymore. The first photo is still revered, but the photographer is the obstetrician who gives his patient a copy of images from the first trimester sonogram.

Maternity clothes have changed, the baby bump is popular, and women display pregnancy as fashion.

Our current culture showers media attention on pregnant stars. Carrying a fetus elevates status, and newborn pictures produce revenue. Michael Jackson stunned the world when he dangled his son from a window for his screaming fans. Jon and Kate Gosselin allegedly had the children in television production for financial support and, of course, months of conversation centered around Nadya Suleman, also known as the Octomom. She was criticized not only for her multiple-embryo pregnancy, which resulted in a total of fourteen children but her decision to allow media involvement in her newborns' lives.

American culture thrives on competition and materialism. Though there is a current trend toward what appears to be an obsession with pregnant women, American capitalistic values of possession, ownership, and success are embedded in parenting. Helicopter parents, or parents who hover over their children and monitor every aspect of the handling of their children's affairs, are a common twenty-first-century phenomenon. Parents curry favor with teachers; team mothers hope to achieve more game time for their children's sports; high school teachers are blamed for failing grades; inappropriate behaviors are excused as poor self-esteem; drug use is referred to as normal and experimental; thousands upon thousands of dollars are spent on adolescent sports in hope of impending sports scholarships and careers, and so on, often to the extent that parents continue to manage their children's college life, employment negotiations, and marriages. Treating parenthood like a business results in adult children who feel entitled and at the same time they lack necessary life skills.

Regardless of what women believe—whether they feel that their purpose is procreation, or that they can have and do it all, whether their self images are linked to the nursery or the boardroom—childbirth is still painful, and the demands of motherhood will emerge. Newborns require care, and pregnancy becomes a memory during sleepless nights, teething, and diaper changing. A being once housed in the female body and nourished by the placenta is no longer physically connected once the umbilical cord is cut.

The first step toward personal development is the mental separation of the parent from the child. Children are not given to us for our personal achievement. They are not born to give us identity as parents who structure the lives of others. For some women, this separation comes easier, but from their first steps, our offspring seek autonomy by their very nature.

Erik Erikson, a psychologist who theorized the stages of psychosocial development, identified this period of separation as beginning at approximately one year. During this phase children attempt basic functions associated with muscular development, such as walking and self-feeding. It is natural for children to develop these skills. When they see themselves progress, they feel confident. Knowing that they can accomplish new skills boosts their sense of self-worth and motivates them to try new things. If their environments are supportive and safe, they explore more. On the other hand, children may develop anxiety and question their ability for future success if environments are unsafe and cause harm or if expectations are too great and they fail. Regardless of their accomplishments or failures, children do start their lives with the desire to succeed. Early in their children's lives, parents have the options to encourage or discourage their natural development.

Margaret is an example of a woman who had no desire to foster independence and mastery in her children. Margaret was born the youngest of ten children; there was a thirty-year span between her and her oldest sibling. Margaret was the baby of the family, and she was definitely spoiled. Because the older siblings married, Margaret had nieces and nephews who were much older than her and catered to her as well.

Margaret's life was typical for a woman of her age. Her family struggled through the Great Depression and World War II. During her country's crises, Margaret married and bore two children, a boy and a girl. When Margaret's husband suddenly died, her nuclear family adjusted. Margaret learned to drive and went to work.

Her first-born child, Jenny, showed early signs of above-average intelligence. She had a gift for linguistics, an unusually broad vocabulary, and a memory that was just short of photographic. Just before her daughter Jenny's wedding and against the advice of family members, Margaret abruptly married a man she had only known for two weeks. Margaret's union overshadowed Jenny's wedding day, and her competitive relationship with her daughter caused others to gossip. In the decades that followed, the family endured problems with Margaret's spouse. He suffered from severe alcoholism, drunken stupors, and gambling debts. His behaviors were so distasteful that he caused embarrassment, separation from family and friends, and ultimately isolation. Every time Margaret's husband disappeared on a binge, her children were expected to entertain and console her. They provided listening and compassionate ears, only to have to pretend that nothing happened when he came home.

As Margaret and her second husband aged, his lifestyle took its toll. He developed diabetes, cirrhosis of the liver, and heart disease. His death was imminent. When Margaret was well into her eighties, she suffered from partial sight and hearing loss, mobility difficulties, severe bouts of dementia, and incontinence. Yet she refused all types of assistance. When social workers knocked at the door, Margaret told them to go away. Meals on Wheels, senior transportation, a medical alert system, and senior helpers were all declined. Margaret insisted that her one daughter care for her. All this time, Jenny believed that she had to honor her mother before all others, and it cost her significantly. Jenny never had any children of her own and ultimately divorced, which made it easier for her mother to burden her. Margaret's demands were clear: Jenny had to be ready and available for Margaret's physical, emotional, and social requirements.

Before Margaret died, Jenny waited for moments of coherency, hoping to hear that she was loved and appreciated. Those words never came. When Margaret died, Jenny and her mother were destructively entwined. Jenny's consistent enabling allowed Margaret's legacy to remain one of self-indulgence and self-centeredness. Margaret had seen Jenny as nothing but an extension of herself, a daughter to satisfy her wants and needs. Jenny accepted this definition of herself and always did what her mother wanted, fearing criticism if she refused. Jenny's opinions were never tolerated, and her intelligence was not respected.

After the death, Jenny had conflicting thoughts and trouble grieving. She loved her mother but also felt deep rage and identity confusion. Sadly, those feelings were a consequence of the lack of boundaries between her and her mother. She was now a woman in her sixties, struggling with the truth that she had allowed her mother to be the obstacle that blocked her from pursuing any of her lifelong goals. Facing her third bout of breast cancer was easier than recognizing that her mother had supported Jenny's own fears of success. Who could she blame now that her mother was gone? Yet, more importantly, who would she be once she was no longer her mother's servant?

Treating our children simply as extensions of ourselves, as Margaret did with Jenny, not only thwarts our children's development, it thwarts our own personal development. Who would Margaret have become without a child willing to cater to her? Perhaps she would have grown from her experience of marrying an addict, realized her fear of being alone, or joined her community for companionship and enrichment. Had such revelations occurred sooner, Margaret might have appreciated the person that Jenny had grown into as an adult; a well-read, self-educated woman. Margaret's life is gone, and those opportunities have gone too. However, Jenny has identified her collusion with her mother, accepted responsibility for her participation, and hopes to find value in her remaining years.

The story of Margaret and Jenny is an illustration of inhibited growth between mother and daughter that reflects on the importance of confronting our life lessons while there is time. Lee, a nineteen-year-old who has observed his friends and their families for several years, has formulated opinions about parents who appear to possess their children.

I live in a middle- to upper-middle-class neighborhood. What I believe is that parents have unrealistic expectations for their children. It's as if they see the children as extensions of themselves and believe that the children have unlimited potential. I've watched my friends and their parents for many years. One parent put so much pressure on the son to be perfect in every way: academically, athletically, socially, personally, even how he handles his relationships with his peers. This friend is now very familiar with the alcohol and drug lifestyle that is prevalent where we live. My friend's father destroyed that kid parenting him. I have another friend whose parents placed high expectations on him, which he is incapable of achieving. He seems to have such a need to be defined by them; it spills out everywhere else in his life. He is always trying to make others happy, tells stories that are half truths, shows up places just to be seen, and brags and boasts, which causes his friends to shake their heads. He behaves like someone who feels inferior. In the last year, he got involved with steroids, and he just doesn't know who he is. He knows what his parents want him to be. Sometimes parents place such expectations on the children that it pushes the parents and children farther apart and strains the relationships. Parents need to know that their kids are just people. Just because they are offspring, they are no greater and no lesser than anyone else. What is important is that your children make it. I define making it as being a good person, finding your spirituality, being successful (not just materially), having respect for yourself, and being proud of yourself. The way parents try to parent creates confusion and misguided directions and skews the path that should be taken. The good intent is destructive. When parents are close-minded, they can be even more unaccepting of what their children want. This is a problem for everyone—the children, the parents, the marriage, and the family. The parents unintentionally set up themselves and their children for failure. Parents need to know that they can only do so much, and the rest is not their job. It is the job of the children.

Chapter 4 — Understanding Emotions

So much of how we understand our environment is based on our emotions. When *Homo sapiens* developed, at first without language, emotions were critical to survival. Humans had to live in groups and only thrived based on mutual interdependence. Before the invention of sophisticated tools, men banded together because hunting and trapping animals required the skills of many. When men returned empty-handed from the hunt, the vegetation gathered by the women fed the tribe. Separating from the tribe or being isolated most likely meant death. Fear was a frequent emotion, as the surroundings held imminent threats from animal and human predators.

Today, the emotions that were so important to cavemen are deeply embedded within us. We have inherited these emotions from our ancestors. Unfortunately, we continue to have emotional reactions to things in our modern-day world that should not be emotionally provoking. For example, today, snakes and spiders are two of the more common phobias, or unrealistic fears, even though humans are much more likely to be involved in an automobile accident or to slip and fall in the shower than to fall prey to a poisonous snake or spider bite.

In the United States, men who show their emotions are often viewed negatively. Male children are taught to restrain their feelings, especially those considered feminine. Consequently, men demonstrate anger as an acceptable social feeling and inhibit behaviors that display emotions like sadness, fear, and anxiety. Females who show too much emotion are commonly perceived as overreacting or out of control, and scientists have researched body organs and hormones to explain it. Even if there are biological causes for these differences, environments where male and females commonly interact discourage emotionality. As recently as 2005, Donald Trump, the wealthy real estate investor, questioned a candidate on his television series *The Apprentice* about crying while she said good-bye to her employees. Trump indicated that crying was a sign of weakness. The contestant, Kendra Todd, offered a noteworthy response. Todd told Trump that she saw linebackers cry after a Super Bowl win and that she was not ashamed. She went on to win the apprentice title of season three; the next time a female contestant cried, Trump did not make an issue of it.

Emotionally based decision making was rejected by our culture long ago. Over the years, our society has embraced scientific conclusions or thinking based on proof. However, twenty-first-century researchers believe that emotions and logic are very much entwined. Though some societies suggest that we should be conservative about revealing our emotions, neuroscientists and other researchers know that good emotional skills increase our chances of success. When we are able to identify our own feelings as well as those of others, we can communicate more accurately. If a spouse is emotionally troubled and the behavior is interpreted as anger, the reactions will be quite different. When we feel remorse about hurting someone, we might apologize. When we believe there is anger, we might respond with more anger. Knowing how to make these interpretations includes studying facial and body language and evaluating the circumstances in which the feelings occur. A joke made in private might cause hurt feelings. A joke made among a group of coworkers might cause humiliation.

When we understand our emotions and know where they come from, we are less likely to make excuses for ourselves or blame others. If we are clear about our feelings, we are better able to separate our emotions from logic and therefore make better decisions. Having emotional intelligence equates to developing these abilities and integrating them into everyday communications and relationships.

When young children cannot identify or communicate their feelings, they often act their feelings out with behaviors that are unacceptable (tantrums, flailing, hitting, etc.). Professionals who work with children utilize their own understandings of facial expressions, muscle tenseness, skin reactions, and social context to assist children in identifying feelings and then associating the feelings with appropriate language. As a result, children learn to express their feelings verbally instead of acting them out.

Most adults are aware of the language of emotion and have greater communication skills than children. Surprisingly, however, without conscious exploration, our typical reactions may not match actual feelings. Processing and understanding deeper emotions are critical for effective communication with others. Because our emotions are legacies of our ancestry, what we feel may not be appropriate in a given situation. Remember, the spider probably won't hurt us, but we react to its presence as if it will.

Another common problem with emotions is that our brains associate feelings with past events. When we remember these events, there is a tendency to react emotionally to circumstances we find similar to the original event. A person might walk on a neighborhood street for years and feel safe. If that person is assaulted on that street, the sight of that street might cause anxious feelings for years to come. Even when we don't remember events, the original feelings can remain. An adult who is afraid of dogs might have been pushed down by a dog at the age of two. Despite the fact that no harm was done and there is no memory of the incident, the negative feelings return every time a dog appears.

Societal rules confuse our understanding or our emotions further, because as we mature, we are trained to disguise our feelings. What we portray as our feelings simply may be a demonstration of what we think is appropriate, not what we actually feel. For example, instead of displaying disgust at a homeless person, the passerby might nod and smile politely.

All of these issues—underdeveloped emotional intelligence, ancestral inheritance, the brain's inability to separate emotion from events, and our cultural rules—make it confusing for children to understand adults and adults to understand children.

Barbara and her son both needed to strengthen their emotional intelligence skills. Barbara and her eighteen-year-old son seemed to argue frequently. Josh wanted to stay out all night, have premarital sex, smoke cigarettes, and drink alcohol. He made it clear that he lied to his mother all of his life because he didn't benefit from honesty. When he told the truth, she didn't like what she heard and punished him. When he lied and was caught, she punished him. Josh chose to lie because it gave him some chance of avoiding punishment. Josh was biding his time until he was able to leave home and become self-supporting. Barbara wanted Josh to be the son she always wanted: obedient, disciplined, honest, and educated.

Barbara and Josh argued, but neither listened to each other. Effective communication requires an understanding of what is being stated, verbally or otherwise. There appeared to be no answer to their dilemma. He was not willing to conform to her rules, and she would not accept his behaviors. As the arguments escalated, each merely continued to pursue convincing the other. Barbara and Josh were similar; both were fierce competitors, and both wanted to win. Josh was old enough to be legally independent, and she could force him out of their house. However, Josh's eviction from the home would neither improve their relationship nor enhance their skills.

When the disagreement began, Barbara expressed anger at Josh's deceit, and he interpreted her response as punitive and controlling. The tenor of the argument changed when Barbara was able to stop and think about what was really going on. Below the surface, Barbara was full of guilt, self-criticism, and hurt. She told Josh that she thought about their relationship every day and could not understand what mistakes she made. She was sure she was flawed. Barbara's existence was tormented by her interactions with her son. After self-reflection, Barbara told Josh what was in her heart. Her voice quieted and her waving arms relaxed. Josh, too, changed, because he interpreted her emotion as shame, not anger.

When Barbara admitted that she found fault with herself, her negative energy was no longer about him but about her. It allowed Josh to see Barbara as a person instead of just his mother. As she expressed herself, she was also able to release her thoughts of self-criticism, which provided her with some relief. The process of Barbara opening up to Josh caused Josh to understand the consequences of his behavior. He realized that he wasn't simply avoiding her rules and her punishments but that his behaviors had caused her pain. That was never his intent.

Barbara's willingness to probe her emotions and communicate those emotions created an opportunity for Josh to empathize with her. Even though she had seen him as unyielding, his refusal to bend helped her admit her deeper and more honest feelings. Their bitter arguing finally had a purpose—it could enhance their ability to communicate with each other.

Some of us understand our emotions quickly and correctly, some of us take more time, and some never understand at all. Some of us let ourselves be governed by and are reactive to our feelings. The reasons for this vary. When individuals do not work to understand their feelings, they lose the opportunity to enhance their lives. Josh, albeit through stubbornness and immaturity, became the vehicle that allowed Barbara to be truthful with him as well as herself, resulting in a more honest relationship. Josh was able to empathize with his mother for the first time in his life at the age of eighteen. Arguably, his empathy was selfishly motivated because he did not want the burden of guilt himself. Nevertheless, he demonstrated greater understanding than he had previously.

Barbara and Josh had been stuck in negative feelings for years. *The Diagnostic and Statistical Manual of Mental Disorders* describes a disorder called rumination. This is the process of regurgitation or bringing up partially digested food from the stomach. This describes what is often done with feelings. We continue to regurgitate them and partially digest them in an unhealthy and unresolving loop that is as destructive as the physical process of rumination. We can ruminate in anger, fear, and victimization.

Barbara was ruminating in anger when she communicated with Josh. She commonly fought with her son, and he always reacted in the same way. Barbara had to learn to interrupt the process so that she could communicate better. When she experienced those surges of emotion, which she believed was anger, she recognized it based on her physical reactions. Barbara's lips tensed, her skin warmed, and her voice became louder. As she leaned toward Josh, she realized that her thoughts raced. Barbara stopped what she was doing and consciously slowed herself down. She thought about her reactions and realized her anger was really about her own shame. She was able to recognize that her physical responses damaged the communication between them. Josh was fighting her, which was not the desired result. She took a minute to define her goals and what she wanted to emote. She considered other ways of approaching him that would cause him to align with her instead of resist her. When she changed her behavior by lowering her voice and talking about herself instead of making demands of him, Barbara was able to see his body language shift. She recognized his discomfort and that it was atypical. He was feeling something he hadn't felt before, which was the empathy mentioned earlier. Barbara's ability to acknowledge her deeper emotions and share those with Josh is an example of emotional intelligence. She identified her emotions, analyzed them, separated them, and monitored his emotions in the context of their argument. The outcome was positive, and Barbara grew from the experience.

Imbalance is another common consequence of reacting based on emotions. Emotions can cause us to overcompensate or let the pendulum swing too far from one side to the other. If a child is treated too harshly, the child may grow up and become a permissive parent. If a child never attaches or bonds as an infant, the child might become unusually close to inappropriate people. Like a coin toss, whether the coin lands on its face or its back, it is still the same coin, and whether it is heads or tails, both are opposite sides. The goal is to balance the coin on its round edges.

The goal with emotions is to seek balance and not to appeal to the opposite extremes. Being too harsh or too permissive are both wrought with their own negative consequences, as are most extremes in emotional life. Children are vulnerable to these extreme reactions, especially if their childhood lacked safety. When adults are explosive or overly aggressive with children, children don't know how to predict what causes that behavior. A slight misstep such as spilled milk or the failure to comply with a request might initiate a series of harmful events. When anything can cause an adult to overreact, children live in a state of war. They are constantly looking for clues that tell them the next battle is coming. This can also occur when children are with adults who have addictions and mental illness. Every situation is an opportunity for an inappropriate reaction, so children grow up and become overreactive adults.

Gina lived in a home with aggression. Her father was very punitive. He was short-tempered and angry as long as she could remember, and as an adult, her childhood friends characterized her youth as a violent one. However, Gina was so accustomed to the aggression, she was surprised by the opinions others expressed about her childhood.

When Gina had children, she was filled with neuroticism. Nothing came naturally to her. She relied on her intellect and began to read, only to discover that she would have to wait for much of life's experiences to show her the way.

When Gina's son was seventeen, she and her husband escorted him by ambulance to an emergency room. His blood alcohol level was three to four times the legal limit. He had been out with the car and was driven home by another drunken peer. A couple of young men tossed him through the front door of their home and fled. As he flipped from consciousness to unconsciousness, he spoke harsh words. He was a self-proclaimed genius. "I could cure cancer if I put my fucking mind to it," he said. "But mostly, I want to do things to annoy you. I want to live a life of revenge just to piss you off." After hearing that, Gina awoke daily with tears on her face. She drove mechanically, wiping her eyes. She couldn't work. For three weeks, Gina felt self-pity.

After years of perceived dedication, sacrifice, cautious decisions, monitoring, pushing forward, and pulling back, Gina was lost. She sought the advice of a therapist, who reminded Gina that he was close to legal age. That scared Gina more. She was afraid that if he left home, his life would deteriorate. The therapist agreed but told Gina she didn't have power. Her son was in control of his decisions, and through his actions, he was making that clear. Gina was told that she was not only afraid for him; she was afraid for herself. Could Gina live with herself if she perceived herself a failure as a parent? Gina realized that she had to stop being the safety net, and her tears fell again.

Gina's son wanted to grow up in a way that best suited him, and as he rebelled (which occurred several times), Gina had an epiphany. She had spent years living in a state of readiness, being proactive and preventive. Her desire for control and her plummeting emotional state came from her overwhelming lack of control as a child. Her past was so full of narrowly escaped disasters that as a parent she refused to let history repeat itself. Moreover, there were overt and subtle characteristics about her son that caused an overlap of identity between him and her father. When conflicts arose, her thoughts shifted from fighting her father to fighting not to be like him. In the privacy of her mind, she often said the words, "Get out." Her father changed the locks on the doors sometime during the year she graduated high school, and Gina never lived in his home again.

Gina recognized the frailty of her human spirit. The emotional pendulum swung from one extreme to the other, from needing to be in control to feeling powerless and helpless. She further understood the incapacity of her own father. Worst of all, Gina had become nothing but a nag. In her efforts to remain one step ahead of her teenage son, she was constantly haranguing. Not only was she exhausted, she didn't like herself anymore.

Gina wanted forgiveness from her son and was disappointed that she embraced those revelations so late in his childhood. But in that process, Gina saw that she had to forgive to be forgiven. She changed her image of her own father; she recognized that he was nothing more than a mortal human being who had strengths and weaknesses just like anybody else. She forgave him. Through Gina's struggles with her son, the forgiveness she found in her heart came years after her father's death. Though an unaware participant, Gina's son forced her to reach greater insights about herself and her history. Had it been someone other than her son, such growth would not have occurred, because Gina would have walked away from others in her life who caused so much pain. This is what makes growth through our children unique—we don't walk away easily or quickly.

Bartholemew is a twenty-one-year-old who believed his parents were overly emotional and therefore too punitive. When they reacted to a drinking incident that he considered typical experimentation, it changed the course of the family.

> When I was fifteen years old, my friends and I planned a night out at a friend's whose parents were out of town. She was having a party, and we were going to be there. Of course, there was alcohol. We planned it all at school. We got a driver and set the details up. The next day, we found out that we were caught. I thought we were responsible. None of us had licenses, but we didn't illegally take a car. We didn't drive while drinking. We found a licensed driver to get us there and back. In my mind, it wasn't that bad of an act. My parents grounded me for months. I couldn't go out. There was no computer, no cell phone, and no television. It was worse than what all of my peers received. I saw my parents as unreasonable and ridiculous. After that, the battle was on. It was a turning point. My parents were so hard on me that it pushed me away. Before that, I cared about what they wanted. I cared about my grades and about my relationship

with them. But thereafter, I did whatever I wanted. I didn't want to be the star kid. I wanted to see what I could get away with. I did stupid things and continued to do stupid things. The goal was to get into trouble. I looked for parties, I looked to see what I could get away with at school; I just wanted to go down the wrong track. I know that I was immature and I know I was dumb, but my parents made a mistake. I wish they would have found a more constructive way to communicate so that I would have comprehended better. It would have saved grief that occurred throughout the next four or five years.

It is unfortunate that our culture continues to encourage the imbalance of emotion in both males and females. Males are often portrayed as insensitive and aggressive, and females are dramatic. Whether it is bra burning, a girl-on-girl kiss, a wardrobe malfunction, body enhancements, a photo of an actress without underwear, dangerous pranks, or extreme aggression and violence, all pander to emotional extremes. We are a society that thrives on shock value, unnecessary enticements, and sexuality. We are so culturally immersed that it is difficult to define normal emotional behavior. This media overexposure is confusing even when we are emotionally grounded and it is difficult not to succumb to its appeal. Though these social influences are challenging, we must work hard to balance our emotions for a healthy existence.

Chapter 5 — Separate the Past

As Virginia Satir, a renowned psychotherapist and Nobel Prize recipient, wrote, "What lingers from the parent's individual past, unresolved or incomplete, often becomes part of her irrational parenting."

As children mature, they often carry the mental framework they developed in childhood into adulthood. This includes an understanding of their role in the family, other familial roles, expectations, coping mechanisms, and unmet needs. The positive aspect of this is that children enter adulthood with a structure or a system. We often hear adults speaking about their understanding of the world by stating, "My mother always said ..." or "My family does it this way." It is helpful to have structures in place that provide ways for us to interpret various everyday interactions. Unfortunately, what we carry into adulthood is not always healthy. Because human beings are habitual, familiar old thoughts, feelings, and behaviors become our adult standards. Coping mechanisms are often impractical because they come from the child's mind and are not applicable in adult life. Running to a parent to tattle on a sibling may be reasonable at ten but will not be appreciated by a parent or a sibling at the age of thirty. Unmet needs are equally problematic. When children have psychological difficulties, they can become emotionally arrested or stuck at a developmental age that corresponds to the period when the psychological problem began. Children can react and respond to those unmet needs and difficulties in adulthood but conduct themselves in juvenile ways. These ineffective patterns often continue even with adults who are aware that this happens.

Stephanie, a trained neuropsychologist, changed careers and started a technology company when she was middle aged. When a vendor she was working with attempted to manipulate and deceive her, Stephanie succinctly put him in his place. Though Stephanie's reaction was appropriate, she described her feelings as "off the Richter scale." Even though Stephanie behaved professionally, internally she was very upset, and it bothered her for days. She thought her reactions were unsuitable and regretted that she had displayed her laser-like tongue. In midlife, Stephanie was unconscious of the lessons of her youth. When she exercised her sharp wit and demonstrated intellectual superiority as a child, her mother made her feel ashamed. Her mother was intimidated by her intelligence and never guided Stephanie in a way that encouraged using that asset beneficially. Stephanie had confused her relationship with her mother with the business transaction. The event with the vendor made Stephanie feel like a child again.

Vera grew up in a home that was never safe. Her father had bipolar disorder, a condition that causes unusual mood shifts from mania to depression, and he was also one of several pedophiles in the family. Vera's memories of childhood were extreme. On the one hand, she thought her mother was perfect. The house was always clean, the meals were always prepared in a timely manner, and the children were polite and groomed. On the other hand, she had seen her nude father mounting her nude five-year-old sister, responded to a screaming brother during an attempted molestation by the father, and watched another sister's repeated sexual victimization by a cousin. Vera did not escape. While her mother found refuge in a weekly class, Vera locked her bedroom door and held her breath. Her father would force his way through, demand duties designated to his wife, and threaten her into silence.

In the early 1970s, Eric Berne's *The Games People Play* provided a paradigm that described a significant percentage of clients seeking therapy. Berne discussed how familial dysfunction establishes itself and is able to repeat itself generation after generation. When children like Vera are victimized, it is only natural that they have certain feelings of hopelessness and helplessness. In Vera's situation she was clearly a victim, and her father was the perpetrator, the person harming her. Because children are dependent, it is a normal to want as well as need to be rescued from the harmful person. Often, children look to the other parent for help. These three personas— victim, perpetrator, and rescuer—become frequently interchanged roles as the victimized child navigates through adulthood. The adult victim seems to shift from one dysfunctional role to the next, always thinking, feeling, and acting like the victim, the perpetrator, or the rescuer.

As Vera struggled through daily life, she kept looking for her rescuer. Her mother, the likely candidate, remained with her father throughout the majority of his life. She encouraged her sisters and brothers to admit the molestation because she wanted validation and support, but it was too difficult for them to relive that pain. Vera also thought she had married her rescuer. He was outwardly impressive, with good looks, athleticism, higher education, and a lucrative career. But he did not want to hear about Vera's past; it was too uncomfortable. He told her that her visible weakness was unattractive. Because he did not like to see her cry, she would wait for him to fall sleep and curl herself into a ball in a corner and sob. The man she thought was her rescuer was emotionally distant and even developed disdain for her.

Vera had fought for herself for as long as she could remember. She battled for life after a premature birth, almost died at five years of age, locked her door to keep her father out of her bedroom, pushed to reveal the family secrets, overcame several medical issues in adulthood, survived a date rape in her early twenties, and more. Eventually, the victimized child became a victimized adult. She maintained all of the damaged familial relationships and flip-flopped between finding excuses for them and blaming them. Vera would say that her mother was just a product of her time and that her father's bipolar disorder caused his sexual deviance. Even her husband didn't have to parent their children because as a professional he had to travel extensively. Not only did everyone in Vera's life have a reason to avoid responsibility, Vera had been victimized at a developmental age that supported self-blame. What happened to her had to have been her fault.

As Vera mothered her three biological children, she combined the needs of her past with her parenting. When that happens, the tendency is to inadequately parent because decisions are determined by the adult's needs more than the children's needs. Because her childhood was so volatile and harmful, her emotions and behaviors shifted radically. Because of her desire to be safe, she isolated her daughter from her husband, concerned that he would molest her. She wanted to be close to her children, so she was an excessively lenient and friendly parent. She was so concerned with her children accepting her that she overlooked their needs, even the multiple signs of her son's addiction. Vera was ill-equipped to objectively see her children's emotional deficits and unable to assist in their emotional development. Each child paid a price as a consequence of Vera's inability to be a consistent parent. One child coped through substance use; the middle child demonstrated apparent rage (which Vera never could); and the youngest was emotionally distant. Vera continued to unconsciously rescue her children by making excuses for them. She enabled them by not holding them accountable and therefore stunted their growth. Vera also continued to weave in and out of the role of victim with her husband.

When Vera was in her fifties, her relationship with her son Thomas took an unexpected turn. Vera accepted that he was an alcoholic, and she went to an Al-Anon group for support. The doctrine was basic. Do not enable the alcoholic; do not be codependent with an alcoholic. In other words, don't become part of the problem. This was so foreign for Vera because in her mind, family members had never been accountable, and the people who became her newfound lifeline encouraged accountability. Vera was told that she should not rescue Thomas. She would have to define boundaries around their relationship, set clear expectations, dismiss her own personal blame, force independence upon him, and expect his failure. Privately, Vera admitted that she would rather have Thomas dead than deal with him harming others while he was under the influence of alcohol. His death seemed a more viable alternative than prospects of positive change.

Holding Thomas accountable, something Vera had never accomplished herself or with others, seemed impossible. If Thomas failed, as seemed likely, the consequences were dire: unemployment, homelessness, incarceration, starvation, or death. The craving to rescue was powerful, but Vera was always a fighter, and she evicted Thomas from the house at the young age of nineteen. As a result, Vera experienced clinical depression and thoughts of suicide.

What happened to Thomas? Thomas spent time at a detoxification facility, and for four years he shifted among sober living houses. Because most homes required complete abstinence, when Thomas relapsed, typically for brief episodes, he had to leave that home and relocate to another.

Today, Thomas is not homeless, or starving, or reckless, or unemployed. He has discovered that he has to work at his life according to the Alcoholics Anonymous doctrine, one day at a time. But just as significant, Vera is closer to Thomas than anyone else in her life. When Vera demanded accountability, Thomas stepped up. Through the honesty of fighting addiction, Vera and Thomas came to know each other, reveal truths, accept mistakes, and forgive each other. Thomas's addiction allowed Vera to have her first honest relationship. It forced Vera to behave in ways that she never had. This was a direct result of her son, and Vera will tell you, "He saved my life."

In marriage family theory, the family unit and its interactions are essential to an individual's well-being, unlike classic psychotherapy, which focuses attention on the individual. The family can have its own identity: each family has a unique structure; it has family members who align together; and it has boundaries regarding interactions. These alignments and boundaries can change often or not at all, but they are considered fundamental to individual family members' dysfunctions. Because of Thomas's addiction, Vera initiated the change in her nuclear family unit. She found a way to bypass her sense of victimization and to create boundaries with a child who could have as easily died rather than rescue himself.

The characteristics that are associated with victimization can sometimes be the most conflicting and confusing identity a parent can have, because the patterns of the parent can be unclear to any untrained person. Parents do many things that children find a way to understand. When children are abandoned, they can create fantasies that soothe the feelings of abandonment. When parents have addictions and illnesses, children can define behaviors as outside of the parents' control. When parents are abusive, children can blame their parents' pasts. However, when a parent behaves like a victim, behaviors can swing from powerlessness and worthlessness to indifference to self-indulgence to anger and more. The child who is exposed to this simply does not have the knowledge that the parent is acting out victim, perpetrator, and rescuing behaviors. As was the case for Vera, the inability of a parent to cope and model appropriate coping strategies can leave a vacuum in children's skills, create emotional distance (because the parent's needs are seen as overwhelming), and lead to inappropriate reactions like addictions and rage. All of these consequences can cause the victimized parent to feel more isolated and more victimized. The parent lives a self-fulfilling nightmare as the children learn to protect themselves in inappropriate ways against the parent's behaviors.

The suffering connected to our pasts, which may or may not include victimization, is often not recognized or appreciated for what it is. Suffering can be a physical, mental, and/or emotional plight, but more importantly, suffering is motivation for change, a motivation that might not otherwise exist. Most of us are satisfied to leave well enough alone even if things are not going well. A past containing suffering can predict a hopeful future. It allows us to appreciate that life offers better opportunities, greater awareness and understanding, and a different way of being. Suffering is a door to the human spirit. The door opens or closes dependent upon the choices of the sufferer.

When adults become parents, they must consciously accept that their children will not heal their wounds, fill the crevices of loneliness, be the primary resources for love and affection, or repair all of the damage from the past. Such repair must be achieved by the adults; if not, the children will continue to present circumstances to encourage that needed repair. When women don't heal from their pasts, they often have more children as they avoid working on their psychological issues.

Lori, a very accomplished woman, needed children to evade feelings from her own childhood. Lori was college educated, attractive, and had attained a high-level position in her field. Her professional life involved managing several thousand employees, most of them male.

Early in Lori's life, she was keenly aware of her mother's disappointments. Lori watched her mother pout and sulk when she was displeased with her daughter. As Lori reached her teen years, she wanted to be more independent and have her own voice. The more Lori spoke up, the more arguments they had. The pouting and sulking always bothered Lori, but they were no longer effective in keeping Lori quiet. Lori's mother lost control and slapped her face, causing skin to tear from under her eye. When Lori's bruises caught the attention of school personnel, they called the authorities for suspected abuse and her mother was outraged.

Lori was close to her father but defined the relationship as emotionally incestuous. There was always an undercurrent of unspoken feelings. Ultimately, Lori believed that she was responsible for the happiness of both her mother and her father. In adulthood, Lori would not betray them. She made bad choices in men, kept her boyfriends away from her father, and never married. Lori became a woman like Jenny in the third chapter, always pleasing her parents. She didn't know who she was outside of her role as a daughter. Even though she was a successful professional, she had little identifiable self. She was a self-described empty shell, a puppet, a person without depth.

Like many women, Lori yearned for children. Her father warned her that he would disown her and repudiate any children she had, but Lori proceeded with artificial insemination. Where the strength came from to make this decision was a mystery to her. After Lori had a boy and a girl, she felt normal. Her children gave her feelings of peace, hope, and happiness. The children made her feel whole.

When her two children were in elementary school, Lori had a decision to make about a possible third child, who she already named Anna Kate. She was an unfertilized egg, and the frozen sperm sat in a vial waiting to be implanted. Lori panicked. She lost focus, couldn't sleep, had nightmares, and wept erratically. Lori was in crisis and didn't know why. All she knew was that she was attached to the idea of this baby being born, though many medical factors suggested that she should not proceed with a third pregnancy. Lori sank into those old feelings of emptiness. Her two children were growing up. At the ages of seven and five, they no longer needed her constant attention and were flourishing. Lori should have been proud of her children, but her parental achievements were overshadowed by torment. Lori's children needed her less, and that meant she would return to nothing.

Lori came to the horrific conclusion that she was using her children for her own fulfillment. Her children allowed her to be aloof with life. She didn't reach out to friends, avoided male companionship, and apologetically told others she only sporadically reviewed her voice mail. Her recognition that she had duplicated her family's pattern of emotional incest with her children was remarkable.

Lori realized that Anna Kate, the infant she dreamed about, seemed so important because she would have saved Lori from the growth and exploration that she needed to pursue. Anna Kate is now a memory, and that egg will never be fertilized. Nevertheless, Lori grieved for her as much as if she had been born. But Lori came to understand that her children could not make her whole. That journey had to be traveled by Lori.

Amber, a nineteen-year-old, believes her family members are dependent on her mother. The intensity of the dependence frightens and disturbs her and in early adulthood, she has already made decisions about her future based on her past.

I am the youngest of three children. My older sister was the star of the family. She did everything right. My brother was a problem. By the time he was sixteen, he stole a car. His grades dropped, he drank and did drugs as well. My parents put all of their energy into taking care of him because he was such a screw-up. I am two years younger than him. What happened to me is that my parents were exhausted from him. They were loving parents, but they had less parenting to give to me. I think that they almost didn't ask me about things in my daily life because they couldn't handle any more bad news. In many ways, I see this as a good thing. I was very much on my own. I learned quite a lot. I was very independent, and when I needed parenting, I found it in my friends' mothers. I became the typical friend that other mothers loved. My parents were always there for me if I needed them, but they didn't look for the relationship with me. I looked for it and I am still looking for it. I make the effort with them, and if I could ask for one thing, it would be that they make some effort to know me. I think my mom is amazing. She has always handled all of the problems in the family. My dad has had some issues over the years. He gambles, withdraws, and suffers from depression. But whatever happens, my mom works with it. When my brother didn't do his homework in school, she took care of it. I am realizing that the women in our family are one way, and the men are another way. It makes me know what I want for my future. I never want to feel the kind of dependence that I see in my mother's life. I don't like it. I think it gets in the way of people growing up. I want to be close to the family I have, and I want to listen to them well. I want to be close to my parents and to my brother and sister. It is important to me.

Amber didn't get the attention that she craved as a child, and she is now vulnerable because of her past. She already has preconceived ideas about men and women. She could marry a man who emotionally distances himself from her or does not support her simply because that type of relationship is familiar to her. Because family is so important, Amber may remain in relationships even after they are no longer healthy. Ultimately, Amber could create her own family and continue to always be the responsible one, confusing independence and control.

Amber is young and has many years to decide how she will define herself. As she learns to separate the emotionality of her past, there is time for her to build confidence in her independence, accept support from others, identify her character strengths, and learn interdependence among family members.

Chapter 6 — Listen with Empathy

People seek therapy because therapeutic conversation is markedly different than social conversation. When people socialize, most of us wait patiently while another person is speaking because we are waiting to take our turn, similar to the way children are taught to share toys. A woman tells a story of an unpleasant gynecological visit, so her friend tells a one-up story about the proctologist. If one person is speaking and another speaks louder, ultimately one of the speakers relinquishes the speaking role. Further, information can be filtered by the listener, who focuses on a small piece of the communication instead of the overall message. This can lead to the listener derailing the intent of the message or responding defensively to the piece of the information that was perceived as offensive. Because of inadequacies in the speaker and/or the listener, these dialogues are often more about personal or social needs than good communication.

Listening is what entices most clients to therapy. Listening is a trained skill. There is no doubt that most of us are equipped with hearing mechanisms that allow us to hear. A movement creates vibrations that are captured and interpreted by the brain. However, listening is not simply the ability to hear; it requires integrating words and their meanings along with other informational cues. Deaf people are able to communicate without hearing mechanisms, but not everyone can listen.

Trained counselors utilize specific techniques that demonstrate they are listening, which ultimately enhances communication. They demonstrate behaviors that can include eye contact, a relaxed appearance, leaning toward the speaker, casually duplicating some gestures, and monitoring their own vocal cadence. Awareness of culture, race, gender, religion, and socioeconomic factors can affect which attending behaviors are suitable for each client. As clients talk, counselors repeat what the clients have said in the counselor's own words to verify the client's thoughts and feelings. If the client appears scattered, a therapist might attempt to clarify or summarize statements to focus the client. Sometimes, a therapist may metaphorically hold up a mirror to help the client see his or her self. Simultaneously, therapists look for inconsistencies between affect, statements, and body language. If a client smiles or laughs after discussing a tragic event, or if a client insists that a relationship is going well while she gazes out the window, a therapist might confront those discrepancies using other techniques. Such processes in therapy lead to the client's deeper comfort and the counselor's improved ability to develop the relationship.

Therapy is about making life changes. When clients have an overwhelming need to be heard, many hours of talk occur during counseling sessions. When children are the source of problems in the family, adults will often relay details of their children's behaviors and conversations. Clients want to let go of feelings they are burdened with. However, the details revealed in conversations during therapy do not necessarily provide critical information that counselors need to develop conclusions about the family dynamics. Typically, this type of dialogue doesn't foster change but is another way of strengthening the working relationship. During these sessions, the client develops trust and comfort so that deeper therapeutic change can occur. Vera, who we met in Chapter 5, had been in counseling for several years. She typically went to her therapist with specific concerns that she wanted to discuss and the therapist obliged her. Because Vera always governed her therapy sessions, her counselor became nothing more than someone who listened to her. Listening caused relief but it didn't assist Vera with the changes she needed to make in her life.

The therapeutic process involves empathy on the part of the therapist. Through training, a therapist can listen to a client and stimulate the same areas of his or her brain as the client's, allowing for a deeper connection to the client's thoughts and feelings. This skill allows the client to feel understood and trust that either the therapist has had similar experiences or has had significant professional experience with similar problems. The therapist, as the listener, always maintains enough distance so that the emotional impact isn't overwhelming. If the therapist becomes too involved with the client, the focus could shift from the client to the clinician. In other words, the professional cannot become enveloped by empathy, because the result would be an incapacitated therapist.

Empathy is not sympathy. Being sympathetic, or feeling sorry for others, is often unhelpful. It confirms that we do not have the power to change what happens in our lives. In interpersonal relationships, we may believe that we are victims or behave like victims, based on prior training and experiences, but more often we create our own helplessness.

With adults, communication problems are listening failures, and listening failures are empathy deficits. Empathy allows one person to imagine what it is to be in another's situation. It is a visceral reaction or a connection to the feelings of another. It is a cognitive reaction, because the empathic person identifies with the thoughts of the other. When there is a convergence of experiences involving an understanding of another's feeling and thoughts, empathy has occurred.

Empathy is natural. Research supports that simply observing facial expressions can elicit emotions in the observer. We know empathy happens not only through vision but through other senses as well, such as touch, smell, and hearing. Research also shows that empathy can elicit both physical and emotional responses in the observer. Haven't you observed panic and consequently felt panic, even if there is nothing for you to panic about? Who hasn't gone to a horror movie to have adrenaline rush throughout their bodies? Physiologically, the same areas of the brain are activated in the observer as the person who is living the actual experience.

Exercising empathy improves our ability to choose positive relationships. First, we reduce our inclinations to prejudge when we create a mindset of learning from and about others. Second, our objectivity increases, because we recognize the information gathered is about the other person and therefore, we understand that it's not personal. Third, we can better discern if relationships are healthy for us. When we assimilate as much information as we can about others, we increase our ability to predict their behaviors because we understand how they view the world. When we know what motivates others, we can better understand their intentions. If we can determine whether someone has our best interests in mind, we can choose to connect with or distance ourselves from that relationship.

Jackie had an interaction with her son that left her disappointed in herself. Her ten-year-old was in the midst of a hockey game and playing poorly. He was in the goalie net and wasn't able to stop most of the goals from being scored against his team. After the first period ended, Jackie's son asked her to meet him at the players' bench. He expressed that the team was playing badly and ridiculed the other players. Jackie interpreted his statements as unsportsmanlike. She told him that participation on a team meant that he shouldn't blame the others. She also pointed out that he was not playing well himself. When the game was over and all of the equipment was off, Jackie's son had more to say. He knew he was not performing well during the game and had needed words of encouragement, not criticism. He wanted to hear "You can do it," and she had let him down; he essentially scolded her. Had she empathized with him, she would have felt his frustration, his personal disappointment, and most importantly, his need for a positive voice during a tough game. Unfortunately, she missed it all.

Not all children are able to deliver such concise and eloquent messages to the adults in their lives, and there is no doubt that Jackie's son was insightful. She was stunned that he presented his disappointment in such a calm and deliberate way that she couldn't help but listen to him. This ten-year-old was able to express his mother's empathic failure. Had Jackie simply utilized some listening skills and paraphrased or reflected upon what he was saying instead of reacting punitively, he may not have played the game any better, but she would have been prouder of herself.

Daniel, age twenty-four, is a bright and successful young man today, but after high school, Daniel developed an addiction. Daniel's parents gave him the independence he needed to learn about himself and patiently waited until he asked for help. When Daniel confronted his problems, his parents empathetically listened to him and provided the support he needed.

> I am a dry alcoholic and am still trying to figure out what that means. My story is probably difficult to hear. My parents didn't really do anything wrong, but sometimes

consequences occur without awareness. I am a typical achiever. I did well in school, both in grades and sports, and still had lots of time for friends. I was popular enough. I was known because I excelled in sports, especially baseball and hockey. By high school, my family moved to an affluent area, which should have been a positive transition. I had freedom and free will. Expectations were always simple: do well in school, work hard, and graduate. When I began at the new high school, I decided to try a different sport. Typically, this would have been a good thing. Unfortunately, the school ranked first in the sport I attempted, so competition was fierce. I couldn't excel relative to the students who played for years. I missed the popularity I once had. When I was admitted to UCLA, I showed up with two handles of vodka. I had good intentions of keeping it all together. I could party, do my premed classes, and join a fraternity. I connected again in a way that I had lost throughout high school, and the social attachments became more important. Within minutes, I was an out-of-control drinker in the darkest way you can imagine. I blacked out frequently, crashed several cars, had driving violations, traumatized family, and made bad moral decisions. Premed changed to a history major because I could show up for class less and cram for tests. Basically, I could pull it off. The alcohol led to cocaine use and gambling, and everything was addicting. I found myself waking up with cigarette burns on my arms in the shape of happy faces. One night I took a heated meat tenderizer and intentionally gave myself a third-degree burn the size of a silver dollar. I self-mutilated and slit my wrist. I realize that I was too immature to be on my own at eighteen. I remember having clear thoughts that I was without supervision and wanted to take advantage of it. My education and living expenses were paid for, which made worrying about daily life a nonissue. Ironically, I ended up abusing that safety net and did have to worry about living expenses and getting through school. What I want others to know is that I am genetically predisposed to addiction from my maternal and paternal lineage. I think that part of my brain is broken, and I have accepted that. I have trouble getting out of bed some days. Other days, I think that if I were gone, lives wouldn't really change very much. I couldn't find meaning in my life and I needed to feel alive. I kept testing and challenging myself. If I didn't die, I must be living for something. Maybe this is why the substance use was attractive. It made me smile, laugh, flirt. It was an instant party. I felt alive when I was high. Unfortunately, the substances didn't help me figure out my purpose. I got tired of waking up with cuts and bruises, having spent my rent money, and trying to figure out how I could get through the day. The lifestyle was exhausting, and I was emotionally bankrupt. By the age of twenty-one, I was sober. My parents could not have stopped this process. I had to go through it before I got better. I had to learn that I am an addict in so many ways. My family was and is the most important thing to me. They support me. The reason I continue living is because I would never want to hurt them anymore than I already have. But I don't learn from others. I learn from myself. My parents told me about my genetics, but it didn't make a difference. I want to say that drinking is too socially acceptable. Parents allow kids to drink too easily, and friends are often allowed to drink in homes as long as they are safe. I've seen parents assume that drinking is a lesser offense than drugs. Most social activities involve drinking, whether it's a beer at a sports event, a rave, a dance club, dinner. Because it's so prevalent, if parents aren't careful, they will overlook potential problems in their children. Just because everyone drinks, and drinks too much, doesn't mean that everyone will escape the danger. Some of us have long-term consequences, and some of us die. My parents may not have been able to stop what happened to me, but that doesn't mean other parents can't stop their children.

The ability to empathize has several benefits. When an adult communicates with empathy, the adult is able to think and feel the way the child does. This level of understanding helps the adult more accurately determine the needs of the child. The more accurate an adult is, the more connected the child will feel toward the adult. When children believe that they are strongly connected, the attachments they experience feel emotional and spiritual as well as familial. The closeness that adults and children can experience, in itself, is a reason to communicate with empathy.

Another important aspect of empathy involves the knowledge that parents and children can be very similar. Children carry 50 percent of the genes from their mothers and 50 percent from their fathers. Children also learn by imitation. Therefore, whether you believe in the idea of nature or nurture (genetic or environmental influences), children will be at least somewhat like their parents, and therefore they are like mirrors. Adults can see themselves by looking at their offspring because some adults can see their personal characteristics more easily in others. For example, when a child is observed teasing another child, a parent might remember his or her own childhood. Based on those memories and a mature outlook, a parent might conclude that the teasing is a result of the child feeling inferior. The parent can remember that teasing was a way of feeling temporarily superior in childhood. The parent then has a choice to confront his or her own personal feelings of inferiority and evaluate whether those feelings have resolved in adulthood. If they haven't, the adult can consider that this is an area that still requires personal growth. Additionally, the parent will determine what options exist to boost the child's esteem.

When adults criticize children's weaknesses, they can confuse children, especially if the children see the same weaknesses in their adult role models. The criticism from the adults can be an empathetic response because adults realize the consequences of those weaknesses—the adults and children have them in common. However, when adults have not been successful in changing themselves, they can think that they are unable to assist and teach children another way. The helplessness the child feels when negatively criticized is the helplessness the adult feels because the adult can't provide the child with more effective guidance. If parents haven't discovered alternative ways of dealing with such weaknesses, they lose the opportunity to improve their own and their children's emotional development. Whether parents criticize or ignore children's deficits, they can delay self-exploration and self-work.

Developing empathy in adult-child relationships doesn't always mean that a parent consciously wants to change when both the parent and the child share a weakness. Parents who see deficits in their children may be very aware that they share the same personal flaws. However, when parents love their children deeply, the sensitivity they feel toward them can allow the parents to judge their children less harshly. What we would otherwise find intolerable in ourselves can be endearing in them. Seeing flaws in children provides adults with the opportunity to be more honest with themselves and to accept their flaws as they accept their children's flaws.

It's important to remember that we can grow through our children when we communicate better. This means that we listen to them with an open mind, from their point of view. It means that we listen with empathy, trying to not only interpret their words but how they think and feel as part of process. When we develop these skills, we can better understand them. When we understand them, because they are part of us, we can better understand ourselves. We then have an opportunity to change ourselves and how we feel about ourselves.

Chapter 7 — Separate Yourself

All adults can learn from children, but parents have more opportunities to learn from their children because the parent-child relationship is personal. Parents actively spend significant time, day by day and year by year, with their children, and the emotional investment in each other is considerable. This chapter focuses specifically on adults who are parents because when adults are actively engaged in parenting, it is difficult to shift focus from the children to themselves. At times, it is hard enough to parent, let alone to try and figure out when children are providing insights for the parents' personal growth. The reality is that most children do not clearly communicate their parents' inadequacies as Jackie's son from Chapter 6 did. Children are typically unable to integrate their thoughts and feelings with the language necessary to communicate such insights. When parents do try to extrapolate information or probe their children, the responses are often defensive or inadequate. As a general rule, when parents recognize that they are struggling significantly with the parent-child relationship, parents should consider there is a need for personal growth.

Children do have different levels of communication abilities, but often they communicate in common ways. Young children may cry and tantrum; preadolescents may lie; teenagers may rebel or ignore us. The different ages and stages include different developmental focuses for children. Infants need to develop trust; toddlers seek autonomy; preschoolers create with imagination; elementary-age children build skills; adolescents learn about their identities; and young adults seek intimacy. As their children progress through these developmental stages, parents should assess whether they themselves have developed the necessary skills that they see their children needing, attempting, or using.

Parents can become very frustrated with their children around twenty-four months of age. This is the terrible-twos period, known for temper tantrums and outbursts. But these behaviors actually develop from children's ability to know their parents from earlier experiences. When infants are born, their awareness is sensory. They see, touch, smell, hear, and taste. Through these senses they create an understanding of the world around them. Before they have formulated language, a harsh touch, a rapid heartbeat, or cold skin stimulates different types of awareness. By the time children incorporate verbal language, they already know their parents from their fundamental sensory identification. That early learning becomes part of their mental framework, and they utilize it to manipulate their worlds as they continue to grow. When children push their parents' buttons, this demonstrates the children's fine-tuned understanding of their parents.

Button-pushing can be interpreted in a number of ways, but most professionals would agree that when a child pushes buttons consistently, the child likes the adult's responses, which are reinforcing, encouraging the child to repeat the behavior. When a child refuses to go to bed and then receives a sermon from the adult about the child's lack of cooperation, the bedtime process is delayed. Though the child might not like the sermon, it becomes a preferred alternative to going to bed. If the child is afraid of the dark, the sermon is more tolerable than the scary monsters living under the bed. The child has found a method of getting his way and becomes the master.

When adults allow their buttons to be pushed, they become reactive to the child. It doesn't matter what it is about: candy at the store, watching a cartoon, bath time, or refusing vegetables. Any behaviors that support a delay or give the child what he wants are successful for the child. But as the child manipulates the parents, mothers and fathers can develop deep, negative feelings toward the situation and the child.

This power shift is uncomfortable and embarrassing. As parents, we all know that we are supposed to be in charge—we should have the final say. For this reason, when the child plugs into the emotional outlets of the parent, significant problems can result. A child who routinely pushes buttons is a signal to the parent. The parent's frustration is related to the inability to discipline or develop cooperation with the child. Frustration is a combination of anger and disappointment, and the disappointment turns toward the parent or the self. These feelings also include lack of confidence and powerlessness. When a parent doesn't recognize his or her personal inadequacies and can only interpret the child's behavior as a battle of wills, feelings can escalate to dangerous levels if the child remains obstinate and the parent has a need to regain control.

Salvatore was a classic button-pushing child. He had developed the skills and knew how to stimulate negative reactions from most adults. Professionals who observed or evaluated Salvatore concluded that he was a troubled five-year-old. In addition to his obvious fine motor, gross motor, and communication delays, Salvatore's social skills were lacking, and he was highly aggressive. He threw objects without caution, ran off the school property, hit others, screamed, dropped himself to the ground, flailed, fidgeted, interrupted, disobeyed, and rarely complied. His outbursts could last from minutes to hours. Though very young, he'd already received psychiatric and psychological services, play therapy, and Head Start, and his mother had received parenting support. He was erratic and petulant, and professionals seriously considered whether he was severely emotionally disturbed and inappropriate for a regular classroom. Salvatore's behaviors caused others, including adults and paraprofessionals, to dislike him, further complicating the situation. This negativity felt by Salvatore is common for children who have severe behavioral problems.

Several events contributed to Salvatore's problems. Before he could talk, his parents separated. His father turned his attention to his new girlfriend's son; his close relationship with his brother changed; he spent too many hours in daycare; and the adults in his life were inconsistent. This was too much for Salvatore to handle. He controlled his world the best way that he could and received attention in very inappropriate ways.

Salvatore's mother had always relied on her husband to discipline him, but when the marriage ended, she did not become the authority in the home. She sympathized with Salvatore because of the upheaval and loss and focused on those feelings instead of teaching him to cope. His exhausted mother experienced extreme frustration levels, but that couldn't derail her desire to improve her parenting skills, as well as herself. Eventually, with the support of behavior specialists, she learned to observe Salvatore, predict his behaviors, listen to him with greater empathy, and constantly exercise self-constraint by separating her emotions from daily behaviors and events.

She had to change, and when she changed, he changed. She instituted boundaries, followed through on what she said, reinforced him when he was good instead of highlighting his bad behavior, spent more positive time with him, and stopped sharing adult problems with him. Basically, she increased her skills, which lead to increased self-confidence. The more she accomplished, the more she believed she was able to do. She developed a sense of mastery in her forties that should have developed during her own toddler years. As a consequence of her enhanced skills, Salvatore became a success story.

The developmental stage between the ages of three and five provides an opportunity for further parental growth. During this stage, children engage heavily in imaginative play, another form of mirroring. Commonly, children observe human interactions in their families and imitate them during playtime. Children will act out the roles of their parents and siblings as they understand them, based on what they have learned. When children play house, the boy might pretend to go to work, the girl might feed the baby, and so forth. Imitative play allows parents to observe how the child has interpreted the family.

Without a doubt, all spouses have negative qualities. Marital partners may not be willing to discuss these characteristics with each other, even if they are problematic. There are several explanations for this. A spouse may fear isolation or divorce from a partner; there is an imbalance of power between them or concerns about being petty. When parents watch children engaged in play, the child's interpretation of one parent's spoken or unspoken feelings toward the other may be revealed. A woman who thinks her husband doesn't help enough might not tell him; instead she bangs cabinet doors and slams drawers while she puts away household items. The child might mimic those passive-aggressive behaviors while playing house.

During the early years, parents may also notice unappealing characteristics of their spouses in their children. A parent might provide corrective criticism to the child, though they don't provide that feedback to a spouse. The child's play behaviors might reflect the uncommunicated changes that one parent wants from the other. A woman might demand excessive cleanliness from a child to compensate for the inadequacies of the spouse. During playtime, that child might shout to another child "Be neater!" as a demonstration of the mother's displeasure with the untidiness that the child and the spouse share.

Children's play activities can reveal opportunities for marital partners to objectively learn about each other, recognize how they treat one another, and potentially identify areas for greater individual development, as well as for improving their marital relationship.

During early childhood, some children display psychic abilities, or knowledge that cannot be explained. There are hundreds of stories about children talking to deceased relatives, playing with imaginary friends, and having awareness that cannot be accounted for in any other way than metaphysical. Many children reportedly have psychic abilities until they develop reasoning. Once reasoning becomes stronger, psychic abilities diminish. Parents who have tried to be open-minded and encourage psychic abilities often lose to the forces of the child's other environments. Gina from Chapter 4 had a son, who said that he would talk to children described as "more than he could count." He talked to them, and they talked back. One night while he was bathing, he screamed in terror. The voices were begging for help, and he panicked. Gina tried to assist him. Shortly thereafter, discussions about the voices waned. Gina's son was between six and seven years old.

Indigo children are children who do not lose their psychic abilities and remain connected to their spiritual purpose, regardless of their age, development, and logic. They are not influenced by their surroundings and are comfortable with who they are and how they understand the world. Indigos are a current-day phenomenon, and there are no scientific studies that show Indigo children are different than other children. Nevertheless, some children do possess unusual characteristics. By definition, Indigo children are born to be teachers and leaders. The challenge for adults who live or work with Indigos is two-fold: Indigos will not conform, and others must be willing to admit that the children know more than they do. When Gina's son was five years old, another parent giggled and said she had taken advice from him and couldn't believe it.

As children age, some parents identify repeated patterns in the household that continue without resolution. These are often general themes, such as disobedience, risk-taking behaviors, defiance, bickering, and disregard. Presuming that the child is not diagnosable with medical or psychological disorders, these behavioral themes are most apparent in adolescence. At that time, parents may be blindsided and unprepared for these challenges, or they may have invested years in attempting to resolve problems that don't seem to go away. Often during this developmental stage, children see their parents' faults, judge their parents' behaviors, and lay blame for parental mistakes. Parenting experts often advise that strict parenting with adolescence can cause greater resistance from the child, resulting in a standoff in the relationship whereby neither parent nor child is willing to change.

Early in life, parents, especially mothers, pride themselves on knowing their children intimately. Each babbling noise is noticed, different cries distinguish needs, and facial expressions make a statement. Once a child reaches the teen years, our society encourages children to wean from the family and establish their own identities. To find this identity, teens experiment with characters that can seem so detached from prior behaviors. As they seek their individuality, it is not unusual for them to try on different styles. Even though they are largely incapable of true separation, they desire independence from their families. During these years real freedom emerges. Teens acquire driver's licenses and cars and often have disposable income from their own employment. Peer pressure and social identification, or social inclusion, often take priority; teens want to be different from their family members. For parents, some of these experimental processes can appear very threatening to the values of the family.

During this stage especially, parents can feel and experience actual loss of control. As parents try to reaffirm the basic fundamentals, like good grades, road rules, and abstinence, teens may push away harder. There can be unprovoked mood swings, blatant anger, and strong intent to physically and mentally separate from the family. Not only is the teen's identity changing, but simultaneously the parent's sense of identity is threatened. This is terribly confusing because adults have identified themselves as parents for many years. By the teen years, the parents have invested so much. For example, when the parents of a good student and athlete discover that their teen is infamously known by the local police, they are no longer the parents of a good student and athlete. They are the parents of a child who may end up in an orange jumpsuit behind bars, which is very inconsistent with the parental image they previously maintained. A strong and successful parent may feel like a failure because of the child's transgression. Perhaps this is why so many intelligent parents ignore their children's problems and excuse their behaviors as normal. The children's safety is equally as important as parents wanting their own identities back.

Teen years can be trying and troubling times. Some teens do dangerous things, and the threat of genuine peril can be very real. Regardless, the more fighting that occurs, the more the parents have to re-identify themselves, reassess values, and redefine the parent-child relationship. Parents have to move from a supervisory to a consultant role, similar to the way businesses utilize such resources. Parent-supervisors give children instructions and monitor the execution of those instructions. Parent-consultants share expertise without expectation that children will embrace it. Basically, parents have to learn that the child is no longer within their control. This is a mental transition, as well as an emotional one. This doesn't mean that teens don't need their parents, and it doesn't mean that a parent should abandon household rules. Rather, this is a time for parents to understand that they must let go and allow their children to find themselves.

When children are minors, parents may seek therapeutic or medical intervention for them. Children can behave in ways that are problematic or in ways that their parents don't understand. Common troubling behaviors include a lack of focus or concentration, motor agitation or fidgeting, failure to follow through, impulsivity, interrupting, forgetfulness, aggression, and regression.

Unfortunately, there is a wide range of causes for these behaviors, which can fall along the spectrum from easily resolved to much more complex: insufficient sleep; improper nutrition; learning disorders; physical, sexual, or emotional abuse; bullying; illness in the family; divorce; lack of proper socialization; substance abuse in the home; substance abuse in the child; and others. Because the most common diagnoses in children do not require blood work or other types of reliable testing, professionals depend on parents for symptom information. Parents are not always accurate, and professionals don't always ask the right questions and/or don't necessarily receive complete information. An incorrect diagnosis can be the result.

It is also not uncommon for counselors to have parents authorize therapy for their children because parents assume that their children need help. In marriage and family therapy, the family member in counseling is referred to as the identified patient (IP). The IP is the person in the family that seems to have the most obvious problems, but other family members are often unaware that they are actually contributing to the problems. There are many reasons to have a child evaluated by a professional, but more often than not, the parent requires skills that are not addressed by sending a child to therapy. This may be a time in a parent's life to slow down and think about how the entire family interacts with each other. Sometimes an experienced parent or grandparent, a wise friend, or seasoned neighbor may be a better alternative than therapy. Salvatore was an extreme example of how a child's symptoms fell under several potential diagnoses. Over the course of three years, Salvatore was tested for mental retardation, learning disabilities, autism, attention deficit/hyperactivity disorder, anxiety disorders, and mood disorders. Ultimately, when his parent improved her parenting skills, Salvatore improved.

Later in adulthood, children make decisions that are often not agreeable to parents. Adult children choose their own partners, education paths, careers, morals, religions, etc. When these decisions do not align with parental values and opinions, the decisions can be viewed as personal attacks against the parents. In that case, emotion can become the driving decision maker. Most of us are familiar with the parental statement, "You're killing me." Though it might be true that our adult children make some decisions simply to inflame us, more often those decisions relate to their attempts at self-development and intimacy.

As parents, our own sense of intimacy can feel challenged as our adult children shift their priorities, take vows with others, and make commitments to their own families. Especially with women, jealousies and insecurities can emerge between a mother and a potential or actual spouse of an adult child. The mother may continue to demand loyalty from her adult child, and the adult child is pulled between the family of origin and the spouse. A mother who does not welcome her child's new partner can feel loss, abandonment, and neglect. Women who have narrowed their social circle or who have emotionally detached from their spouses can feel especially isolated without the companionship of their children. This can be a critical juncture in a woman's life because an adult child may create distance from parents if pressures from the family of origin interfere with daily life. However, becoming an in-law or a quasi in-law is an opportunity to develop new relationships. It can be the chance to have the daughter or son that was never born, as well as to correct regrets. As adult children create their families and extend their relationships, mothers can expand the circle of companionship. Every new relationship has the possibility of creating greater empathy and deeper connections, which in turn leads to personal growth and greater self-awareness.

The different developmental stages discussed in this chapter provide some illustrations of periods in children's lives when their behaviors might signal an opportunity for parents to consider turning their focus inward as well as outward. Parents should listen with greater emphasis and consider the potential for personal growth in these phases. They are opportunities for self-improvement. They can be enriching. They can be healing. As parents we want to always teach our children. How we do so changes over time. We teach through role modeling. As we mature, this is achieved through our ongoing development.

Chapter 8 — How to Change

The chapters in this book have described areas of awareness that adults have to consciously develop in order to benefit from lessons that children can offer. However, knowing that we need to grow equates to changing ourselves, and often adults just don't know how to accomplish that. For example, we may realize that we should increase our patience, but somehow we continue to lose our tempers. The reality is that it feels better when we assess the acts of others, regardless of whether those critiques are positive or negative. When we focus on another person's behaviors, we ignore our own behaviors and are distracted from self-development. Also, it is simply easier to be objective with others. We can view their interactions as we view a performance or read a book. If we are good at it, we can predict with some accuracy what the next scene or next chapter will reveal.

When we try to be objective with ourselves, we have to question whether we really are the person we have convinced ourselves that we are. This is difficult to do. Are we who we think we are? Do we present someone different than who we really are, or are we sometimes who we think we are and sometimes not? Do these perceptions change over time? These questions that we must answer for ourselves assist in the development of self-awareness, but the shift from objective to introspective is time consuming, confusing, and sometimes painful. Fortunately, introspection that leads to change is possible; we all have the potential to alter characteristics in ourselves, and an ability to execute change is a vital life skill.

At twenty-one, Sam knows herself. She understands how she felt as a teenager, why she felt the way that she did, and, perhaps most importantly, how to communicate those thoughts and feelings so that she is heard. The road to that knowledge was difficult for all of her family members, but Sam would say it was worthwhile.

> I have an amazingly awesome relationship with my parents and couldn't be happier. When I was sixteen years old, however, this couldn't have been further from the truth. I had a horrible relationship with them. The problem was simple; I was queen of the world, and they failed to recognize it. Several events took place that caused me to change. I was the only one of my friends with a car, so I used it to tow around all my buddies and ditch school. I was never into alcohol or drugs even though some of my friends were; however, being the naïve teenager that I was I still chose to hang with those who were. My parents were never the super-strict parents that you'd imagine; they gave me lots of freedom. I was educated in private schools, and in my junior year of high school I decided to try public school. Public school gave me more freedom than private schools did, and I simply couldn't handle it. I took advantage of both the school's freedom and the freedom given to me by my parents. If my parents let me go to a concert, it wasn't enough; I wanted to stay out all night, do what I wanted, and not let them know what I was up to. Eventually, I (an accident, mind you) crashed my car into a friend's house, which led to the big life-changing event—being sent away to boarding school.

This wasn't just any boarding school. This was an all-girls' boarding school for those with mainly drug and alcohol problems. I had to be tricked into going because I never would have gone willingly. It was in another state than my family; it was a nine- to fifteen-month program, and I wasn't allowed to talk to anyone from home. My friends assumed I fell off the face of the earth. I had to do individual and family therapy. I stayed at the school for thirteen months before I graduated the program. I had immense hatred and anger toward my parents for "taking my life away," but now I couldn't thank them enough for saving our relationship. My parents and I had a communication problem. They didn't understand why I was so angry and pushed them away, and I couldn't understand why they always told me what to do. They were looking out for me; they are parents after all. If I was being punished, yelling wasn't the way to go. Yelling made me defensive, and in that mode I was unreachable and unpredictable. It's safe to say that I and my parents are stubborn hotheads. Once we learned how to channel our feelings and intensions without yelling at each other, well, it became easier. I think if more parents took the time to understand their children as opposed to simply trying to protect and keep their children close, they'd get a lot further. The same goes for the teenagers. If they could speak to their parents without yelling or having the whole "my way or the highway" stance, everyone would have a better understanding and better communication. Being sent away for a year was an extreme measure, but necessary. It's not always that way. During therapy I not only learned a lot but my parents did as well. Sometimes going through the motions of being a good parent isn't actually doing the job of being a good parent. Sometimes we all just have to take a step back and listen. It worked for my family.

We know that the change Sam's family went through was stressful, and prolonged stress can be harmful. To reduce stress, it's important to establish daily routines that include some type of relaxation. Relaxation actually helps the brain stay focused, goal-directed, and motivated. Some relaxation techniques include meditation, yoga, diaphragmatic deep breathing, and progressive muscle relaxation, or tensing and relaxing muscle groups.

After establishing stress-reduction routines, we have to change the way we think and/or the way we feel. Changing our thoughts requires reminding ourselves of the goals we want to achieve, replacing old thoughts with positive ones, and reinforcing new thoughts that are more productive. For example, when we diet, a note on the refrigerator helps keep us on track. When we have negative thoughts (like quitting the diet), we have to hit the stop button on the tapes that repeat in our thoughts. The negative sections have to be erased and replaced with thoughts that are aligned with what we are trying to achieve. When the dieter loses two pounds, even though four would be better, she gives herself credit, because two pounds is better than none. Like buying a new outfit, reinforcing ourselves for replacing the old thoughts, encourages us to maintain our efforts. When we consistently remind ourselves to replace unproductive thoughts and reinforce ourselves for doing so, we create new routines that help us to not only initiate but to maintain change throughout our lives.

Altering our feelings can occur in several ways; the most obvious way is to change our thoughts. A second method involves the mirror neurons in the brain. When mirror neurons are stimulated, we connect with what we are observing. If we see facial expressions and body language, we relate to the feelings associated with it. If we want to change our feelings, we can observe the desired feelings in others. The observation is processed in the brain similarly to a personal experience; it causes us to feel the emotions we perceive coming from the person being observed. Once we feel it, we have to practice it until it becomes habitual. Neurologically, we are actually using imitation to change feelings. We observe the feeling in others, and then we can know it in ourselves.

Virginia Satir was known for working with clients and their families through role play. When her clients took on the personas of other family members, they would speak, move, and even breathe like the person they were imitating. Her clients realized that acting as if they were someone else caused them to think and feel differently. They became the essence of the family member they pretended to be. The experience allowed family members to understand each other when other attempts at communication failed. When the clients felt differently, their behaviors changed toward their family members.

Another strategy for changing our feelings is to observe ourselves. When we are aware of a particular feeling, we can look into a mirror. We can look at our own facial expressions and body language and associate our demeanor with that feeling. When we repeat those expressions and body language, we can repeat the experience of the feeling. It is typical when we change our feelings to realize that our thoughts have shifted too, because our thoughts and feelings are intertwined.

Carrie is a mother who intentionally changed her thoughts and her feelings as a desperate and last alternative. Carrie was surprised when her teen daughter, Sam, began dating a drug dealer. Mother and daughter were close, so when Sam revealed this relationship, Carrie was ambivalent. Carrie appreciated Sam's honesty, as always, even if the information shared was disconcerting. When Carrie met

Sam's friend, her intuition and instincts reacted, and Carrie knew the young man would cause problems. Within months, her tall, head-turning athlete of a daughter seemed to disappear. Sam became a daily drug user, with all of the characteristics of an addict.

Carrie wanted to save her daughter; failure was not an option. She scrutinized cell phone records, instant messages, and e-mails as well as spied with surveillance equipment. Nothing was unreasonable, even sabotaging the boyfriend's vehicle or planning his untimely death. What was once insane became feasible. Carrie had lost her mind.

Carrie, a model in her youth, married an engineer and educator. She made people feel at ease, and she was a natural problem solver. She was also conscientious, value driven, intuitive, creative, and altruistic, and her personality profile placed her in the company of great leaders like Mahatma Gandhi, Martin Luther King, and Nelson Mandela. When her first child was stillborn and the doctors could not explain why, she vowed that she would never lose another child again.

When Carrie decided that Sam was in real danger, she drove to Sam's college town and rented a room nearby. When she met Sam for dinner, Carrie didn't recognize her except for her eyes. Carrie was too late. Within twenty-four hours, Carrie went home, and she wanted to die. Everything that Carrie had believed about herself in her adult life—her ability to protect her children, her drive to have authentic relationships, her desire for the truth—was challenged. She found herself among intricately woven fibers of deceit, which is what happens when one is intimate with an addict.

Carrie had a decision to make about the future relationship she would have with Sam. Carrie decided that everyone loves a baby, so with clear intent, she envisioned a marriage, meeting in-laws, and a pregnant daughter. She transformed everything fearful and made it digestible, even the distasteful association with a liar. Carrie changed her thinking. She made a dramatic shift from trying to save her daughter to professing that she had no right to tell others how to live. Carrie stopped judging. It was a critical life lesson. She stopped snooping and accepted that Sam was in charge of herself. The decision and the process were painful.

Carrie had unintentionally extended Sam's rebellion. Had Carrie continued her interference, the destructive interaction might have lead to death. However, because Carrie demanded change in herself, she was better able to reconcile whatever the future held. Shortly thereafter, Sam implemented her own changes. She began exercising again, dropped the loser boyfriend, and terminated the drug use. Carrie is an example of change that was finite and demonstrative. She reduced her emotional reactivity by altering her negative feelings and replacing her thoughts. Carrie was motivated to change herself because she believed her daughter was at risk. Her relationship with Sam underscores the power of our children and their capacity to move adults in directions they never would have gone.

Every time we change ourselves and try to improve, we grow. Personal growth builds our own self-esteem and confirms to us that we are able to confront new challenges. When we have been successful in the past, we know that we can be again. But perhaps more importantly, when we change—whether it is our thinking or our feelings—we teach our children, because we are their role models and they learn from watching us. When we give our children a method of coping in life, we better prepare them for the challenges that inevitably come their way. If we want our children to change, we have to be willing to actively show them how.

Chapter 9 — Forgiveness

The stories of the women in these chapters share a basic theme: they are often troubled, to the extent that they are thrust toward movement away from their pain. Their pain comes from the unique relationships that they have with children. They are willing to change. Before that happens, they have to forgive themselves.

Adrienne spent several years in a Catholic elementary school, which required church attendance and occasional trips to the church and the confessional. The confessional entry was a thick velvet curtain that covered a dark, narrow booth, separated by a mesh window, with a priest waiting on the other side. Upon entering, the confessor would say, "Bless me, father, for I have sinned." Adrienne would make up sins because she never remembered what her actual wrongdoings were. "I lied three times (well, now really four), and fought with my sister twice." Absolution was granted after prayers were said—Hail Mary for the lightweight sins, and Our Father and the Act of Contrition for the more serious transgressions.

Many Catholics who understand Canon laws do not understand the comprehensive intent of confession, but when it is fully implemented, it is purposeful. Confession is not simply leaning on a kneeler, having sins recorded, saying a few prayers, and assuming that forgiveness has been granted. Confession is a more complex process. It demands acknowledging your sins, recognizing their harm, and feeling heartfelt sorrow or repentance, along with a sincere desire not to commit those sins again.

Accepting responsibility that you have done harm toward someone or something else is synonymous with empathy. When you have a clear vision of your actions, a heightened awareness of the thoughts, feelings, and subsequent behaviors of the one who received the transgression follows. It is this level of empathy toward another that the Catholic Church suggests permits God to forgive. This forgiveness returns the soul to a state of grace, which affects the soul's destiny.

Unfortunately, in American culture, forgiveness is a misunderstood concept, because the emphasis is placed on the offender expressing sorrow. At a very early age, a child is taught to apologize, which is the act of asking forgiveness. Responsible adults who demand that a child says "Sorry," leaves the recipient feeling jilted when the "sorry" is delivered without sincerity or doesn't arrive at all. This type of exchange gives more power to the offender, who gets to decide if, how, and when the apology is given. Apologies never rescind the act, turn back time, erase pain, or release a victim from future emotional trauma. It is a nicety. Saying "Sorry" is polite and socially acceptable. Saying that you forgive someone who has apologized is the appropriate social response. It is typically understood that when there is honest sorrow, the offender makes the changes necessary to ensure that behaviors are corrected. The proof is in future acts, not in the verbal apology. Consequently, people who often apologize without making meaningful changes are seen as confused, in denial, or simply untruthful to themselves and others.

True forgiveness is an individual and private act. It is a decision-making process that allows the recipient of the wrongdoing to compartmentalize and diffuse the emotions connected to a painful event. Forgiveness is a choice to discharge the negative emotions, push through the obstacles associated with the event, and consciously demand that control of the self be internal. True forgiveness is never about absolving another, forgetting that it happened, or sanctioning the event. It is the ability to move forward with life because without forward movement, the wrongdoer maintains power.

When life events require true forgiveness, forgiveness includes self-evaluation. It is normal to question our actions and second-guess our decisions. These critiques can be fueled by blame and self-doubt. Uncomfortable feelings are to be expected but what is important is the recognition of what could have been done differently and incorporating those changes into future decisions. When learning occurs from live events and we observe changes in our patterns, self-doubt diminishes because there is awareness of success—that another step has been reached in personal growth. If this process does not occur, insecurities will continue to drive future decisions. In other words, decisions will be based on increasing feelings of security. These will be safe decisions but they don't encourage growth. Feeling safe generally doesn't motivate change because if it's not broke, why fix it?

People who suffer from addictions exemplify decisions based on safety. When a person uses alcohol, the substance is a way to cope. It works because the addict escapes painful thoughts and feelings. After prolonged use, alcohol has side effects and causes other problems that can significantly impact life. Addicts can lose their families, homes, and employment. When those losses become obvious, sobriety becomes a better alternative. The event or events that are too high of a price to pay for drinking are personal to the individual. For some it can be a divorce, an overdose, an automobile accident, or a death. Whatever the event, the motivation to change and stop drinking becomes less painful than losing family, friends, and more.

This is when the addict will leave the security of alcohol and attempts significant changes in thoughts, feelings, and behavior.

Similar to confession, the path to forgiveness is through the empathetic process. Empathy lets us realize that the wrongdoing is not about us but about the human condition. People rape to control, not because the victim deserves rape. People defraud for capital gain, not because others deserve to have less. Every misaligned act that wrongdoers commit is about their lives—their perceptions, their histories, and their excuses.

Forgiveness does not mean that relevant events should be dismissed or ignored. However, in order to forgive, it is critical that we learn about whom we were and who we can become from such events. This is the greatest opportunity for personal growth. We often hear about family members who create foundations or lobby for new legislation based on tragedy. Such people live forgiveness daily—they move forward with their lives and create positive change. John Walsh, host of *America's Most Wanted*, founded several centers along the East Coast that eventually became the National Center for Missing and Exploited Children. He lobbied and testified before Congress many times before successfully securing votes for the Adam Walsh Child Protection and Safety Act; he participated in nationalizing the Amber Alert system and continues to advocate for victims. His lifelong work and multiple contributions grew out of the abduction and murder of his young son.

The Law of Attraction is a centuries-old theory that regained popularity when Rhonda Byrne authored *The Secret*. The Law of Attraction suggests that we have control of our thoughts, which affect the decisions we make, which determine whom we surround ourselves with, which ultimately affect the quality of our lives. The concept suggests that we create our physical world based on our thoughts. Some of the controversy around this best-selling book has to do with its premise, which infers that victims are at fault for their own challenging circumstances because victims are, in fact, the masters of their universe. What we believe becomes reality. The attraction theory supports that people who believe in powerlessness find themselves in powerless situations. It is difficult to support that bad things happen to people because of a mindset and in that way, Byrne expanded this concept beyond what many consider reasonable. As long as we live typical lives, we are not immune from pain. However, implementing empathy and applying forgiveness to ourselves and others are the building blocks to achieving the Law of Attraction. This is why forgiveness is so significant. When we let go, we can think about what we want in our lives instead of thinking about whom or what has been wrong. Forgiveness allows for a mental and emotional path that is based on positive instead of negative thinking.

Perhaps the most meaningful journey is that of forgiveness between a parent and a child. The world of young children is narrow. Their parents are the center of their lives. Children are dependent and attach themselves to the parent who is meeting their needs, regardless of the parent's personal shortcomings. When parents are tired, frustrated, angry, or confused, children can misunderstand such feelings and, more importantly, the actions associated with them. Many children have the innate ability to forgive their parents, but they can also interpret their parents' behaviors as being directed personally at them. Although a parental behavior might affect the child, often the parent is simply unable to do better in that moment.

The perceptions about their parents that young children develop can become hardwired. These perceptions can become tightly woven into how they interpret others in the world. Children can hold on to the pain caused by a parent for decades. This agony can even survive the death of the parent. Quite often, the adult child has little awareness that childhood has had such an effect. Because of the inherent imbalance of power between a parent and a child, the child can grow up with a sense of being harmed or victimized over events that a parent may not even recall. As children mature and progress through adulthood, as they strive for independence and their own identities, they often continue to make decisions based on the precepts that were formed earlier in their development. Unfortunately, the conclusions that we arrive at when we are children are derived from an immature brain that can reduce complex situations to basic concepts that are incorrect.

Donna's early childhood impacted her relationships for decades, because unbeknownst to her, she had made some decisions as a toddler. Donna's mother married a man who captured her heart but abused her. After Donna and her sister were born, Donna's father spent more years in prison than free. Donna almost didn't remember him at all, but her mother said that when Donna saw him, she looked through him, without emotion or acknowledgment. One of Donna's few memories included her older sister dialing the rotary phone, begging to speak with her "Daddy," and then hanging up. Donna saw her sister sob, and Donna decided that she would never be so vulnerable. By the age of four, she had emotionally shifted beyond hate to apathy. As far as she was concerned, her father was dead.

While Donna was developing spoken language, she had already determined how she would live her life: as a classic overachiever. Nothing and no one would be an obstacle for her. In adulthood, she became accomplished in several professions: as a buyer for a major department store chain, a licensed embalmer and funeral director, a beauty contestant, a stockbroker, and a real estate agent. She was beautiful, fit, elegant, and fashionable. She was also tortured.

Donna became a master of dissection. When Donna was hurt—as she inevitably was—every associated, minuscule element of that event had to be understood to make sure it wouldn't happen again. Because Donna was so bright and so articulate, words were her sword, her demeanor was her shield, her history was her fortress, and her buried memories were her militia. In her efforts to defend and protect, she alienated others and withdrew.

By the time Donna was in her forties, she had a reputation that she didn't understand and she didn't like. Her ex-husband, her ex-fiancé, and her son all said she was tough. Donna wasn't tough at all. She was simply protecting herself from the gender that she believed could destroy her. Donna always became defensive and went into the self-preservation mode she adopted when she was three.

Donna might have continued on, never fully understanding who she was, but fortunately, Donna had a son. He let Donna know what he thought about her: she was always looking for a fight; she was dismissive of his feelings; she made him too nervous; and she didn't listen. He didn't want to be around her anymore.

One night, Donna and her son had words about her parenting. He shouted that she wasn't listening. He shouted that he had to get away from her. He showed disdain, and Donna cried. She couldn't believe that her own flesh and blood could hurt her this way. He was the only male in her life that she was vulnerable with, and he cut her to the core.

The next day, he entered Donna's room, covered his face with his hoodie, laid his body across her, and sobbed. This experience was different for her. When Donna stopped feeling sorry for herself, she decided to change. Donna stopped fighting and quieted herself. She let her ex-husband have more of a parental voice and gave her son more space to grow. The more she stepped back, the more the relationships improved. Most importantly, Donna realized that the man who she had ignored and labeled as insignificant, her father, had influenced her life greatly. For more than forty years, she had been unaware, but she finally understood.

Donna's son was suffocating from his mother's hostility. At sixteen, he was too immature to understand the complications of her life.

My mother always seemed angry. It didn't matter what it was about. It just never stopped. When my parents divorced, I felt like the fighting that had taken place between my mother and father shifted more toward me. It was as if I replaced my father. The anger in the house affected me. When I was younger, I was too nervous to respond. When I got older, the arguing escalated out of control. But past that, the fighting made me feel that I wasn't good enough, that I didn't do enough, and that I could never be enough. I had so much stress inside, these arguments ruined my days. I would simply leave. I couldn't stay around it and realized I could walk to my father's house and talk to him. I had to get away from it. I think the arguments were because my mother was afraid. She was nervous that I would interfere with the opportunities I was given in life. I also don't think she trusted me to handle my own life. Now that I am older, I know that my mother taught me life skills. The strict parenting kept me on track and taught me to take care of myself. The arguing has quieted, so I think my mother is changing. Our relationship feels better. I am happy to see my mother and happy to spend time with her.

Parents like Donna can have great difficulty identifying and admitting that they made mistakes while raising their children, regardless of whether the errors are minor or critical. When we are unable to forgive ourselves, our energy is wasted as we protect our mistakes and bury the truth. We live with defensiveness and denial and as parents refuse to honor the truth, the children build and exaggerate resentments.

Most children, including young children and adult children, want to forgive their parents. They want to let go themselves and alleviate the pain they feel toward their parents. Chris, a twenty-one-year-old, resented his parents from early childhood. Then he watched them forgive each other and him, which assisted in his own personal growth.

I realized certain characteristics about myself by first or second grade that shaped my outlook for the next several years of my life. When my parents tried to expose me to something they thought would be positive, I saw them as trying to control me. I always thought that if they had done these things when I was younger, it would have been part of me. Even though it doesn't seem possible, by age seven I thought they were too late.

As I grew through elementary and middle school, I saw other peers get things that they needed for the sports they played. I played those sports but never got those things. I interpreted the lack of new and better equipment as my parents' refusal to give me support. I was angry most of the time—angry because I didn't get things and angry because of how I perceived my parents. My parents failed me, so I gave up on them. By high school, too many people around me were doing bigger and better things. It didn't take long for me to realize that there was money in selling drugs.

I was already using them, so the distribution was easy. I was a social person, and my communication abilities gave me entry everywhere I wanted but saved me from places I didn't want to go. I was sent to the principal's office weekly because I always smelled of weed. I was stopped multiple times by the police. I could have scales, drug paraphernalia, and bags of product in my car, but ultimately I would just drive away. I'd been arrested, stood in front of judges, and mostly received warnings. My parents would lecture me, but I think they were afraid. If they came down harder on me, I would have rebelled even more. When they demanded that they drug test me, I just ran away, for days at a time. When I came back, I cleaned my system enough so that I tested only for weed, and they were relieved. I was unstoppable. After high school, I was hired by a major bank and within months I ranked at the top of my department. Life was good. I was making $35,000 legally and much more with dealing. I dabbled in college and turned my classes into more drug sale opportunities. I wasn't learning; I was dealing. It was one man and one act that changed me. By the age of twenty I was fired because my friend was getting high in the parking lot of the bank on a daily basis, and I didn't report it. I thought I was fine because I was driving off the property when I got high. I was still working hard and handling the business I was hired to do. My employer said I wasn't looking out for the company or myself. It was days before Christmas; I didn't receive my bonus, and I was broke. All this time I thought I was bettering myself, but I was actually falling. I was a frog in a pot of boiling water. I was warm and comfortable and didn't realize I was cooking. I looked around and saw my peers going to school, succeeding toward graduation from college. Comparatively, I was an unemployed, hostile, drug-using dealer. The employees at my job were all in their forties, without education, unable to meet their expenses. That was my path. There are things that I did that I am not proud to have done. I was so high on cocaine that I tried to punch my father with a closed fist. My brother, who looked up to me in a bigger-than-life way, followed my path of drugs. I disrespected many people. Throughout it all, my parents fought about me, and they never gave up, even if I did. They stayed together, and they held our family together. I know what effort that took. My family doesn't communicate well. I tell my father I love him, even though I don't hear it back. It would be nice if he could give that to me. I needed better boundaries. The simple truth is that this one insignificant man who fired me was the first person who ever stopped me. Two weeks after he did it, I got the message, strong and clear. I wasn't bigger than life, and I had to be cut down to size. Don't get me wrong. I have great self-esteem and think that I have places to go. Life is nowhere near over for me, and I plan to live every day without fear. But as a kid, it was just too easy for me to go wayward. I needed my parents not to be afraid of me. I needed my mom to believe her words meant something. It gave me too much confidence and too much freedom.

I am sorry for the things I have done and am atoning daily. I am trying to correct my relationships, especially with my family. I love them and I forgive them, and I know they love and forgive me, too.

When parents don't hold themselves accountable for their acts, they and their children can become polarized, each expecting understanding from the other. The interplay is stunting. Neither learns and neither grows. What parents must remember is that children teach us that we make mistakes. They point out our shortcomings. They sometimes know us better than we wish to know ourselves. When parents forgive themselves, they teach their children to forgive. When parents forgive, they let go and release themselves from the past. Forgiveness is a bridge. It allows for movement between where we started and where we can go. Those possibilities are as great as we are willing to imagine and as possible as we are willing to create.

Chapter 10 — Disabled Children

It is often unknown why children are born into our world with significant challenges. There was a time when children with developmental disabilities such as mental retardation made up a small percentage of the population, and within that group the majority of children were higher functioning. However, today, developmental disabilities are on the rise, and most parents fear the possibility of autism. Once uncommon, autism is now diagnosed more than many other early childhood disorders.

Parents who have developmentally disabled children come to know the world quite differently than parents with typical children. Being told about potential defects or deficits in young children is often traumatizing. One woman gave birth to twins who were so premature that neither was expected to survive. With other babies at home and the prospect of two disabled infants, this mother secretly wished for the death of one of the infants. Those feelings of despair speak to her state of mind, which was fear that she was incapable of an apparently daunting task. Another woman, as she struggled with her child's neuromuscular disorder, was told that her son might have autism. She said that she would rather die. When his diagnosis was confirmed, she learned to handle his difficulties in quite a courageous way. The first diagnosis was difficult enough, and this parent needed time to adjust to the other. Most of us hear about these disabilities through organizations that attempt to raise awareness and funding for research, treatment, and cures. However, personally, parents who live with developmentally disabled children grieve. It is simple to suggest that parents care for these children; doing so can be lifelong.

Before the age of three, diagnosed children may receive a barrage of early intervention services, including speech, physical, and/or occupational therapy; floor time or child-directed play; behavior intervention; assistance with social development, and so on. Parents have been primed that early intervention is crucial, so daily life during early childhood shifts from one appointment to the next. When there are other children, balancing the needs of the family can be overwhelming.

How parents handle the demands of such disabilities varies. Some parents rely on professionals and paraprofessionals, and others find these resources inadequate. Parents may discover that their child's needs are supported, but dealing with the system can also lead to feelings of frustration and defeat. When children have disabilities that are rare, the terrain may be new for parents and professionals. Determining what services are appropriate can occur by basic trial and error.

When Lorraine realized that her son was atypical, she sought medical advice from the best educational medical facility in her area. At the age of three, he was diagnosed with ADHD and was prescribed an amphetamine. The doctor never recommended a follow-up visit, and by the age of four her son exhibited symptoms she couldn't ignore. He arranged foods and toys in a methodical order, refused to use the toilet, defecated in the backyard when he defecated at all, stuttered, and demonstrated a laundry list of what appeared to be unusual sensitivities. His days seemed to be predictable. By midafternoon he was agitated, and by early evening he was out of control.

What Lorraine didn't know was that her son was experiencing a rebound effect. As the medication wore off, his symptoms became more aggressive than his symptoms had been without the drug. The amphetamine prescribed was not recommended for children as young as three. When a behavior consultant questioned the diagnosis and treatment, Lorraine sought other medical opinions. Her son experienced such severe encopresis (withholding of bowel movements) that one doctor could feel the fecal impaction by touching his abdomen. It was the size of a grapefruit. He also had autism, and the amphetamines exacerbated the eating and sleeping difficulties common with that diagnosis. Once the proper assessments were conducted, Lorraine realized that she had to find a stronger voice. Her fantasy of living in her gingerbread house gave way to reality. It took years for her to accept that she had to fight for services, and as much as she tried to maintain positive relationships, she was forced to hire advocates. Lorraine was never the same. The new, strong voice she developed for her child was well suited to other areas of her life. She learned to accept disapproval from her parents, judge herself based on her own values, and establish guidelines for her personal relationships.

The outcomes for developmentally disabled children range from positive to very negative. Some children remain in regular classrooms and have the same expectations for achievement as their peers. Others are in regular classrooms with a separate curriculum designed for their individual needs. Some reach adulthood and remain with their families throughout their lives. Others live independently with the assistance needed for daily skills like budgeting and grocery shopping. Opportunities for work also exist—with systems that allow competent workers to transition from sheltered environments to unsupervised employment. Social activities with others can include trips, dances, and other outings that are available in the region of residence.

The other end of the spectrum can include developmentally disabled who are coddled, pitied, or isolated. Depending on the age, they can be literally warehoused in different environments and positioned in front of cartoons. Social interaction with the mainstream population can be attempted but rarely do children and adults of average intelligence befriend others who are visibly developmentally disabled. Integration into the world as we know it is never seamless. It can be even more difficult for higher-functioning children; when intellect, motor functioning, and communication appear normal, professionals can and do overlook other symptoms such as overstimulation, unusual sensitivities to sounds, lighting, textures, and touch, high levels of anxiety, obsessive thoughts, and compulsive behaviors.

Parents can become hyper-vigilant, learning laws, enrolling in seminars, and hiring advocacy in an effort to provide every possible opportunity that might have a positive result for the child. Family resources are spent trying the next promising treatment, like mercury detoxification, special diets, and hormone therapy. These remedies become popular through media buzz, but they can have diverse outcomes because their efficacy is not proven. Parents, in their desire to achieve the best results, may not recognize the consequences of their efforts. Their children are often lonely. The saddest circumstance is when a higher-functioning though disabled child recognizes that he is too low-functioning for one world but too high-functioning for another.

Developmentally disabled children easily attract predators. Both males and females are molested at rates far higher than the average population. Their social needs, coupled with their cognitive deficits, give predators easy access. Because the developmentally disabled make poor witnesses in court, their abusers are often unpunished.

The developmentally disabled share the rights that all citizens have: freedom to spend their income (even foolishly), to engage in risky sex, and to abuse alcohol and drugs. Those who work closely with this population can attest to the range of problems that occur when legal rights do not align with maturity and judgment. Parents who attempt to maintain control are forced to seek legal conservatorship or to ask a court or law to shift basic rights from the developmentally disabled person to the parent. If a person is not severely disabled, seeking to take his or her legal rights is difficult. Parents can find themselves trapped if their children are too high-functioning to be legally conserved but are still low-functioning enough that others easily take advantage. Unfortunately, the very laws that were designed to protect civil rights have done so at a cost; they have unintentionally burdened others who have the moral responsibility of their children without legal authority.

We may never understand the purpose of children born with difficulties. People view such life events differently. Some believe that there is never a justification for a child to be born to struggle in life, or worse, to never have the awareness of existence as we know it. Some view these struggles as a gift and some as a punishment. There is no question that the weight parents often bear can cripple them, destroy marriages, and affect siblings. Though the divorce rate in the United States is high, it is higher among couples who have developmentally disabled children.

Parents who best handle these challenges create communities when their children are young. They navigate through the various school and daycare environments, find children who have skill levels complementary to their children, connect with other parents, establish safety nets, and develop social networks that work. They maintain a balance, meeting their children's needs in light of the reality of who their children are. They reduce their own anxiety and fear and increase their knowledge of their children. They utilize the various available resources and support systems, continue open communication with those outside resources, and at the same time maintain their own voices.

Developmentally disabled children are special. On one end of the spectrum, they appear like other children, and at the other end of the spectrum, physical and mental deficiencies are obvious. Some are very difficult to reach. The children that appear unreachable require intense sensory awareness of subtleties such as their breathing and eye focus. Adults who invest in developmentally disabled children, regardless of the severity of disabilities, change as individuals, parents, and community members. This is why developmentally disabled children are here. It is through these children that we learn who we can become. The parents who raise such children and other adults who dedicate themselves to this population can become our moral leaders, a gift offered to the rest of us who struggle with our daily lives. We live in a period of time that represents high divorce rates and fatherless babies—an overall lack of commitment to family and each other. The developmentally disabled require, and at times demand, that commitment that our society has made less important. We live during a time that encourages instant gratification and the developmentally disabled remind us about hard work and hardship. We live during a time in which materialism is associated with and expected to create feelings of well-being. The developmentally disabled remind us of the simple pleasures. Perhaps most important, we live during a time when love is based on personal wants and needs. The developmentally disabled remind us that deep love can come from giving.

When a therapist met with Annie, she couldn't imagine how to provide psychotherapy services. Annie was a severely disabled teenager in a motorized chair. Annie did not vocalize, barely used a communication board, and had a feeding tube. Her body was frail and dysfunctional. The therapist was told that Annie had drastically shifted from a happy person to someone with symptoms of post-traumatic stress disorder and depression. All the adults around her, and there were many, testified to her metamorphosis. Annie is an example of a child who did not speak but impacted many others.

Without the possibility of verbal communication, her therapist had to rely on other skills. She observed Annie at length in her home, at school, and in daycare. Over time, the therapist recognized that Annie exhibited different behaviors in each environment. She would never wet herself in settings shared with her peers, but she stopped signaling her toileting needs at home. She flailed and appeared to have horrific flashbacks at school but not at daycare. Annie learned much more than suspected. She was an adolescent who recognized that she could get away with much less work than she was capable of, and she did. After the adults in Annie's world stopped attending to and reinforcing her problematic behaviors, all of the problematic behaviors stopped.

Annie was a girl who got two reactions when she was in public: people stared or turned away. People like Annie rouse very uncomfortable feelings in most of us. Yet the Annies of the world require significant empathy and concentration. When we learn to invest enough energy trying to understand people like Annie, we come to understand people who are less challenging much more easily.

After the presidential campaign of 2009, Sarah Palin was accused of calling her son retarded. Mental retardation is, in fact, a legitimate diagnosis, used to refer to a level of intelligence and ability to adapt to everyday functioning. When she reportedly called for the resignation of a White House staffer for using the same word, he was using the word in the common vernacular. People often use the word *retarded* to suggest oddness or stupidity. Some of us find that word offensive. Some of us are indifferent. Such usage and interpretations suggest a gap in understanding or empathy among us.

Those who live in the world of the developmentally disabled must learn to embrace it. Those who live outside of the world of the developmentally disabled do not have experience in it. Cardinal Roger Mahoney said, "Any society, any nation, is judged on the basis of how it treats its weakest members—the last, the least, the littlest." This population elicits different emotions from different people. Fortunately, many have compassion for the disabled. Some of us are afraid of what we don't understand. Others can have discomfort. The developmentally disabled, as a community, have the unique ability to reveal the human spirit with its positive as well as negative qualities. In this way, this community holds up that reflecting mirror so that we can better observe ourselves. When we see ourselves, we have the opportunity to grow and this is the contribution they offer.

Chapter 11 — Conclusion

This book, meant to cross the boundaries between religion and culture, was not written to offend anyone's sensibilities. All of us should recognize the importance of children in our lives. The goal of this book is to awaken people to the fact that our children have potential beyond what we realize. We need to understand that children are more than an impression of our genetic codes.

Children are born to develop their own identities, and they have their own personal destinies. It is difficult for parents to separate their destinies from their children's because their lives are closely intertwined. However, it is through this combination of genetics, learning through imitation, and close proximity that children have energy which is similar to adults. This results in children knowing their parents well. This bond creates an opportunity for adults to learn from children, especially parents. When this learning occurs, adults can rewrite the mistakes of the past and learn new ways of relating to each other. Healing can result and growth can occur.

The intertwined steps discussed in this book overlap. When parents are emotionally out of balance, it's usually because their emotions, which often spring from unresolved issues in childhood, are triggered. If not careful, parents can look to their children to soothe their discomfort or to place blame. Consequently, parents always have to be mindful of who they are and who they are not.

With conscious effort, parents can make the changes needed to grow. This requires that they forgive themselves, because without forgiveness, they will continue to be emotionally triggered.

The truth is that as adults, we sometimes unintentionally hurt children—our own and others. Our egos interfere with being educators, our competitiveness overrules our judgment, and our drive escalates so that we step on others' backs to raise ourselves. These are aspects of human frailties that appear as we live and work with children. None of us are immune, and if we could be more forthcoming about these weaknesses, more adults would be compelled to openly seek help. The women's stories in this book suggest that even the bright and the educated experience angst with their children. Often, the more angst is felt, the more desire there can be to change the children. However, such experiences further suggest a greater need for the adults to develop.

There is no shame in feeling lost, especially when children make decisions that are adverse to ours. Children have their own life courses that they have come into the world to pursue. These courses may not be in sync with what others want. If they were, we would be living our dreams through them.

Children are an energy force that comes into our world through mothers. Based on theories in physics, energy is not created or destroyed but simply changes form. Human desire to procreate doesn't grant us choosing rights regarding the energy that comes through us. That energy that becomes a human being is given to us for unknown reasons. The energy we call our children becomes part of our family based on societal and cultural dictates.

We do not have to apply the past to the future. We simply have to understand that we can create something different. Creation is an element of the mind, not the brain. The normal mind is limitless in its potential, which means that the parent-child relationship is limitless in its potential. It is bound only by beliefs that we refuse to change.

Recognize that your children are not here so you can repeat the past; they have the capacity to create growth for themselves and their parents. Face your parent-child relationships with confidence. Agree to take charge of who you are, and know that your emotions are determined by your own beliefs. Allow your emotionality to have its rightful place in your life; feeling is a life asset, but being ruled by feeling can be a liability.

Learn to listen to children. Empathy is the path to effective listening. When understanding children is combined with an ability to listen, communication becomes less selfish, and parents become more available. Though it is true that children need our guidance, they can guide us as well. Take time to rethink communication, and listen for messages that may be inherently designed for your own growth. The level of parental struggle likely correlates with the messages and life lessons that we as parents have to absorb. If parents can reach this level of empathy with their children, they will attain another level of self-awareness. Uncomfortable thoughts and feelings can accompany those insights. Through the act of forgiveness, we can let go of the toxicity and focus our energy on improving ourselves. Through these processes, we in turn teach our children who they can be.

As adults, we should realize that parents should look for common ground with children as well as look for differences. Their life cycles and their developmental stages are the same, and their problems elicit similar emotions. Herein lays the danger of wanting them to become us and to replace us. The genetics between parents and children can encourage replication. Therefore, we must underscore that children may be an integral part of our destinies but have their own destinies as well.

This book incorporates several psychological theories, along with other disciplines. Utilize these theories to make positive change and create personal growth. There can be a negative bias toward psychology. Psychological explanations have been used to explain or excuse behaviors that would otherwise be unforgivable. In spite of these negatives, the ability to understand yourself and others can be achieved through psychological methods. Because the focus of psychology is change and growth, by definition psychology means growth, and the practice of psychology inherently resides in all of us.